SELF-DEVELOPMENT FOR SUCCESS

Effective communication

Acknowledgments

The following have contributed to the preparation of
this book or to the development of the approaches
taken in it:
Sheila & David Roebuck
Dr. Paul Dobson; City University Business School
Stephen P. Robbins

SELF-DEVELOPMENT FOR SUCCESS

Effective communication

THE ESSENTIAL GUIDE TO THINKING AND WORKING SMARTER

Chris Roebuck

AMERICAN MANAGEMENT ASSOCIATION

Dedicated by the author to Sheila and David Roebuck

AMACOM
American Management Association
New York • Atlanta • Boston • Chicago • Kansas City
San Francisco • Washington, D. C.
Brussels • Mexico City • Tokyo • Toronto

A Marshall Edition
Conceived, edited, and designed by
Marshall Editions Ltd.
The Orangery, 161 New Bond Street
London W1Y 9PA

This book is available at a special discount when
ordered in bulk quantities. For information, contact
Special Sales Department, AMACOM, an imprint of AMA
Publications, a division of American Management
Association,1601 Broadway, New York, NY 10019.

This publication is designed to provide accurate and
authoritative information in regard to the subject matter
covered. It is sold with the understanding that the
publisher is not engaged in rendering legal, accounting,
or other professional service. If legal advice or other
expert assistance is required, the services of a
competent professional person should be sought.

Library of Congress Cataloging-in-Publication Data
Roebuck, Chris, 1956–
    Effective communication / Chris Roebuck.
        p.   cm.
    Includes biographical references and index.
    ISBN 0-8144-7020-3
    1. Business communication.   I Title.
HF5718.R633 1999
658.4'5--dc21
                                98-53812
                          CIP

Printing number

10 9 8 7 6 5 4 3 2 1

Series Consultant Editor Chris Roebuck
Project Editor Jo Wells
Design Martin Laurie
Art Director Sean Keogh
Managing Art Editor Patrick Carpenter
Managing Editor Clare Currie
Editorial Assistant Sophie Sandy
Editorial Coordinator Rebecca Clunes
Production Nikki Ingram

Cover photography The Stock Market

Originated in Italy by Articolor
Printed and bound in Portugal by Printer Portuguesa

Contents

1

Achieving objectives
Inform people
Inform yourself
Develop skills

Is effective communication important?

Will better communication benefit me?

How can I improve my skills?

Why Is Effective Communication Important?

The ability to communicate effectively at work and in life is perhaps the most critical skill for anyone. Without communication nothing can be achieved. It is communication that holds our society together; without it, we are just individuals relying on our own experiences to help us through life. The ability to communicate – to pass on ideas, experiences and feelings – has allowed the human race to develop.

Imagine the impact on your family and all the problems that it would cause if, suddenly, you were unable to communicate with each other. Phone messages would not get passed on; chores would not get done; and money would be wasted, as you and your partner duplicated the weekly shopping.

An organization is just a group of people; and, if the members don't communicate effectively, the same problems arise that would occur if a family did not communicate.

Poor communication leads to poor performance; yet it is common in the workplace. Happily, communication skills can be improved; and, the more effective the communication, the better the overall performance and the greater the level of achievement.

Team Leader
Planning • Organizing • Controlling • Motivating • Developing

Downward Communication
Flow of Plans • Instructions • Expectations

Feedback
Upward flow of Communication • Results • Expectations • Views and Ideas

Individual or Team
Performance

The same applies to individuals. The more effective you are at communicating, the more likely you are to achieve what you want. Communication links the different stages when you do anything – from playing a game of football to chairing a meeting. In order to achieve your objectives there needs to be a flow of information in both directions.

Effective communication allows you to use all the other skills you have to the fullest. The ability to motivate, delegate, organize, solve problems, and obtain information all rely on your ability to communicate with others. Unless you can communicate well, you will find it very difficult to be effective at work or even in your personal life.

Over 80 percent of our waking life is spent either sending or receiving information. To help you understand how important communication really is at work, write a list of things you do in your job that entail some communication. For example, taking and passing on a telephone message, writing a letter and contributing to a meeting all belong on your list. You can stop if you go over 25! Can you think of anything you do at work that does not include some communication?

Communication is a two-way process. In addition to getting your own message across, it is also important to listen to and understand what others have to say – a technique known as "active listening." This will ensure that you can give other people what they want, while at the same time, getting the information you need to do your own job.

Allowing other people to communicate effectively with you is just as important as communicating effectively with them. For example, if your boss never bothered to listen to you, you would probably become very demotivated; and things might start going wrong as a result. If your boss did not listen, your problems (perhaps a lack of resources, late deliveries from suppliers, difficulties with other departments, or simply stress) would remain unknown and, as a result, ignored. Without asking how things are going and listening to the reply, he or she will not even know whether you have accomplished the tasks that have been assigned to you.

It is important to realize the potential effects a lack of communication could have on your performance and that of the organization.

You already know from experience that poor communication can cause problems. How often have you been given unclear instructions by your boss? Have you ever misunderstood what colleagues are trying to say? How often have you asked somebody to do something in a way that you believed was quite clear and then discovered that they misunderstood you? How many times in the last week has there been some form of communication problem at work? What consequences resulted?

Will Improving My Skills Produce Benefits?

Effective communication can transform how well people work. Imagine an organization in which everyone is kept informed, knows exactly what to do, and has all the information necessary.

Think of a workplace where your ideas and suggestions are welcomed, other people offer you their help and knowledge, and there is never any confusion, rumors, or worry about saying what you think about the way things are done.

THINK OF A GOOD COMMUNICATOR

Think of examples of bad communication that have happened in your life. Note five incidents of bad communication you have experienced. Try to identify what went wrong and the consequences.

Also, think about individuals you have known who were good communicators – maybe a boss or a teacher. Give examples of their effective communication, how you benefitted from the experience, and how it helped you to work better.

Writing down experiences of both good and bad communication, what made them good or bad, and their benefits or consequences, will help you focus on how well you communicate. Think about the experiences you have written down, and ask yourself, "Do I do it this way?"

Sharing knowledge is critical to success. If, rather than keeping quiet, people shared their knowledge with others, the experienced helped the inexperienced, and problems were solved using everyone's knowledge, this would dramatically speed up the skill development of less experienced people. It would also allow more delegation and facilitate problem solving.

Just think of the energy, freedom, and enthusiasm that such an organization would encourage. Now, think what effect it would have on the performance of the organization if everyone felt motivated and empowered. It would be a great place to work. This is what effective communication can achieve. In the real world some companies have realized this and have invested a great deal of time, effort, and money on improving their communication.

Bad communication, in any form, carries the risk of wasting time and resources because the wrong thing being done or causing conflict between people. Both reduce the team's ability to get the job done and can cause lasting harm if relationships break down. Evidence suggests that bad communication is probably the cause of most of the problems people encounter at work.

THE COSTS OF BAD COMMUNICATION

People aren't clear about what they should do, which leads to wasted time and wasted resources.

People misunderstand what is being said, which leads to bad working relationships.

People don't communicate ideas and knowledge, which leads to slow skills development and problems that take a long time to solve.

People don't know why they are doing things.

Staff morale drops, which leads to high staff turnover.

The organization is unresponsive and inflexible, which leads to a negative image with customers and clients, as well as a loss of business

BENEFITS OF EFFECTIVE COMMUNICATION

Everyone knows what they should be doing.

Everyone understands why they are doing what they do and how this fits in with the organization's goals.

The resources are in the right place at the right time.

You have all the relevant information to do the job.

Any idea that can improve performance will be welcomed and used.

People learn and develop skills faster.

Problems are solved quickly, using all the knowledge within the organization.

The organization is flexible and can respond quickly.

How Can I Improve My Skills?

Even though you may already be a good communicator, everyone can improve on their current abilities. Even if you assume that you communicate well, it is likely that you rarely, if ever, assess how well you actually perform. This is your opportunity to see how well you are doing at the moment and to improve your skills where required.

Improving how you communicate with others is much easier than you think. In many ways you already have a lot of experience communicating. You have been involved in social communication since childhood. This will have helped you understand some of the basics; but, for effective business communication, these existing skills must be fine tuned in order to get the message across in the best way and achieve your objectives.

In chapter two you will be able to assess how you are doing in all the major areas of communication you encounter at work. Chapters three and four will help you understand how to communicate effectively in these areas, put together a plan to develop your skills, and show you how to improve the communication skills of all of the members of your team.

You can build up your skills across the major areas of communication, from writing reports to using the telephone. Use the self-assessments, ideas, and checklists, in order to regularly assess how your skills have developed and to help you in the future. The way you will improve your skills is by using simple formats that you can transfer effectively to work situations. In addition, you will be able to understand the principles behind how the communication process works. This will

Build On Your Experience

Regularly Assess Your Skills

allow you to be effective in situations that may not be covered by this book.

The most effective way of improving is to assess your skills, which are based on your previous experiences, identify and improve on your areas of weakness, and capitalize on your strengths. This approach will allow you to target the time and effort that you put into developing your skills, concentrating on areas where it is really needed – and where it will bring the most benefit. This process will also accustom you to organizing your own self-development so that, in the future, you can take control of your own development as it becomes necessary. You may assume that your organization will take care of your development; however, many organizations do not do so or, at least, not in the most effective way. You should be aware of your own needs so that if the organization does not develop you fully you can plan your own improvement.

Being a good communicator is a joy, not a chore. Getting your ideas across, helping other people, and achieving your ambitions all come with effective communication. Think of a time when you have helped someone overcome a problem by giving them advice, and the satisfaction you obtained when the problem was solved. Communication made that possible.

That new team member you helped to become an expert in some area, the time you helped your boss appreciate the benefits of delegating more responsibility to the team, the first team meeting you successfully ran when your boss was away – all of these were made possible by effective communication. If you invest the effort to develop your skills, the benefits will be substantial.

Capitalize On Your Strengths **+** **Improve Your Weak Areas**  **Communicate More Effectively**

2

Self-assessment
Strengths
Weaknesses
Feedback

How well do I communicate verbally?

Am I a good listener?

How good is my written work?

Why Is Self-Assessment Important?

To improve your skills you have to know how good you are. A general self-assessment will enable you to identify your strengths and weaknesses. Then you can plan ways to improve. Each assessment focuses on one area of communication.

Check whichever of the suggested answers best describes what you do. The assessment process will only benefit you if you are honest. At the end of each section analyze your answers, and hone your understanding of your own skills.

Face to face with another person

Most communication is carried out face to face with other individuals: asking for information, offering advice, your annual performance appraisal, or telling someone what you think of their performance, all tend to be done in a one-to-one situation. This is one of the most critical areas of communication to get right. With a little help most people can greatly improve the way they communicate one to one. Assess how you are doing at present.

	Question	usually	sometimes	seldom
1	Do you find that people get the "wrong end of the stick" and misunderstand you?			
2	Do you find that when you are talking to others you lose the thread of what you are trying to say?			
3	Do people come back and ask for further clarification of what you have said?			
4	Are you ever sarcastic?			
5	Do you avoid using face-to-face communication?			
6	Do you try to phrase what you say and deliver it in a way you think is appropriate to the person you are talking to?			

How Did You Score?

Questions 1–5		Questions 6–12	
Usually	1 point	Usually	3 points
Sometimes	2 points	Sometimes	2 points
Seldom	3 points	Seldom	1 point

More than 32
Your face to face communication skills seem to be good. There may be room for improvement in some areas.

26–32
You have some skills, but you could use considerable improvement.

Under 26
Your skills need substantial improvement in many areas.

	Question	usually	sometimes	seldom
7	Do you maintain eye contact when you speak to someone?			
8	Do you ever ask the person to whom you are talking whether he or she has understood what you said?			
9	Do you try to find an appropriate time and place to talk?			
10	Do you ever tell people why you are asking them to do something?			
11	If what you need to tell someone is difficult, complicated, or both, do you plan it first?			
12	Do you ask people for their views?			

Face to Face With A Group

Communicating face to face with a group of people can be an intimidating thing to do, whether it is a group of new customers or the people that you work with all the time. In such a stressful situation it is easy to forget things and make mistakes. It is probably the most intimidating form of communication you have to do, but it can be a valuable way of providing information to everyone or soliciting the opinion of a wide range of people on one particular issue. It also means that everyone is getting the same information, which removes the potential for confusion.

As a team leader, you need to be effective at communicating with a group - that's what your team is. With practice even the most nervous person will be able to address their team. Don't try to avoid doing it. If you follow the advice given in this book, you will be able to create a structure you are familiar with and can rely on. When it becomes automatic, you will have beaten your nerves and may even start to enjoy speaking to a group. Feedback is just as important when you are talking to a group as when you are talking to a single person. So, plan some time into your agenda to answer questions and to ask for opinions from your audience.

Question	usually	sometimes	seldom
1 I am nervous about speaking to a group.			
2 If we have to hold a team meeting, I let the team know about the meeting well in advance.			
3 Some team members don't contribute to meetings.			
4 I plan in advance what I am going to say at any team meeting.			
5 In team meetings I do all the talking.			

How Did You Score?

Questions 1, 3, 5, 7, 8, 10		Questions 2, 4, 6, 9	
Usually	1 point	Usually	3 points
Sometimes	2 points	Sometimes	2 points
Seldom	3 points	Seldom	1 point

More than 26
Your direct communication skills in a group seem to be good. But there may be room for improvement in some areas.

20–26
You have some skills, but you could use considerable improvement.

Under 20
Your skills need substantial improvement in many areas.

	Question	usually	sometimes	seldom
6	After I brief members of my team, they never ask for more information or clarification.			
7	I let people speak as much as they like at meetings.			
8	I let people argue to clear the air.			
9	I always ask if there are issues people want to discuss other than mine.			
10	I always treat each group of people I speak to in the same way.			

Giving Feedback

If you want to manage other people effectively, it is essential that you give them feedback. Most people's major complaint about their bosses is that they are rarely told how they are doing on a day-to-day basis. Most say, "I'd rather know if I am doing badly; at least I'd know one way or the other."

If you don't give feedback, how can people know that things are going wrong, or (hopefully) well? Giving positive feedback (praise) is easy; it is the negative feedback that we all try to avoid giving. Don't fall into this trap. The team would rather know than not know. How can they improve if you don't tell them? It is essential to deal with problems as soon as they arise with well-planned negative feedback, rather than allowing the problem to build up.

It is also essential in terms of motivation to let your team know when they are performing well. Give praise where it is warranted.

	Question	usually	sometimes	seldom
1	I focus my comments on specific job-related events.			
2	I keep my comments descriptive and subjective, rather than using evaluations or figures.			
3	I prefer to save up comments so that they can be presented and discussed in detail at the person's annual performance review.			
4	I always ensure that my feedback is clearly understood.			
5	I supplement criticisms with suggestions on what the person can do to improve.			
6	My feedback focuses on the person's past performance and not on future potential.			

How Did You Score?

Questions 2, 3, 6, 9, 11		Questions 1, 4, 5, 7, 8, 10, 12	
Usually	1 point	Usually	3 points
Sometimes	2 points	Sometimes	2 points
Seldom	3 points	Seldom	1 point

More than 32
Your feedback skills seem to be good. But there may be room for improvement in some areas.

26–32
You have some skills, but you could use considerable improvement.

Under 26
Your skills need substantial improvement in many areas.

	Question	usually	sometimes	seldom
7	I always try to find something positive to say, even if there are negatives.			
8	I always ask for the other person's views on my feedback.			
9	Rather than getting into a discussion, I always tell the individual concerned what kind of behavior to expect in the future.			
10	I ask people for their views on their performance before I give them mine.			
11	I find it difficult to give negative feedback when I should.			
12	I give praise if someone has done well.			

Using The Telephone

The telephone is one of the mainstays of modern business communication. Everyone uses the telephone, but not everyone uses it well or at the appropriate times.

To get the maximum benefit from the telephone you must be sure that you use it to benefit yourself and to help those who call you. When you place a call, you can help the person at the other end do what you want by handling the call effectively yourself. The success or failure of the call depends just as much on the way you approach the other person as it does on the way he or she responds. When someone calls you, he or she will have an objective. If you can help the caller achieve this objective, you will create a positive impression of you and your organization. For example, if a customer calls to order some equipment but is not sure what is needed, and you provide assistance, that person will be pleased with the outcome of the call. A telephone conversation requires more concentration than a face to face meeting because you do not have the advantage of signals from body language to help you understand the message. No matter how inconvenient it may be, devote your full attention to the call for the few minutes that it lasts; and take notes to ensure that you remember the key points of the conversation.

	Question	usually	sometimes	seldom
1	I let the telephone ring at least five times before answering.			
2	When I answer I give my name, department, and ask how I can help.			
3	To save time I often read memos or letters whilst on the phone.			
4	When calling other people I always ask if it is convenient for them to speak.			
5	I always try to keep the call short, even if it means interrupting the caller.			

How Did You Score?

Questions 1, 3, 5, 7, 8		Questions 2, 4, 6, 9, 10	
Usually	1 point	Usually	3 points
Sometimes	2 points	Sometimes	2 points
Seldom	3 points	Seldom	1 point

More than 26
Your telephone skills seem to be good, but there may be room for improvement in some areas.

26–32
You have some skills, but you could use considerable improvement.

Under 26
Your skills need substantial improvement in many areas.

	Question	usually	sometimes	seldom
6	I ask for clarification if I don't understand what the caller has said.			
7	If the call is long or complex, I find that I sometimes lose track.			
8	I never bother to write down messages because I remember them.			
9	I update and check my voicemail or answering machine regularly.			
10	I always write down what I have to do right after the call.			

Written Communication

Many people are nervous about committing themselves to paper. Anxiety about making mistakes with punctuation, spelling, and grammar should not prevent you from using the right type of communication to get your message across. In many cases, this is written communication. It may take more time than a conversation, but putting your thoughts in writing can have the advantage of forcing you to really think about what you are saying before your message reaches the other person.

You have probably said something and then thought, "Hang on, that wasn't really what I meant to say," or "Oh dear, that wasn't a very intelligent comment."

With written communication you have more chances to get it right. Be sure you use them.

It's a common misconception that a written message should be more complicated than if it were delivered face to face. This can lead to long-winded letters, which only confuse. Stick to clear language, avoiding jargon the other person will not understand. Keep it simple and logical, and you are more likely to be successful.

Keeping a written record of complicated communications can be invaluable. How many times have you had to refer back to a message or information source?

Question	usually	sometimes	seldom
1 I avoid writing things if I can.			
2 People come back and ask me to clarify what I have written.			
3 I plan what I am going to write before I start.			
4 I send off the first thing I write.			
5 My written communications are full of long and technical words.			

How Did You Score?

Questions 1, 2, 4, 5, 8		Questions 3, 6, 7, 9, 10	
Usually	1 point	Usually	3 points
Sometimes	2 points	Sometimes	2 points
Seldom	3 points	Seldom	1 point

More than 26
Your written skills seem to be good, but there may be room for improvement in some areas.

26–32
You have some skills, but you could use considerable improvement.

Under 26
Your skills need substantial improvement in many areas.

	Question	usually	sometimes	seldom
6	All my written communications are clear and concise.			
7	I ask a colleague to check important documents I write.			
8	I never use written communication if I can speak to the person concerned.			
9	People understand what I mean when I send them things I have written.			
10	I think writing a report is something I could do without problems.			

Listening Skills

One of the most important parts of communication is listening to what other people have to say. If you don't, you will miss out on crucial pieces of information. This information may be about things that are going wrong, things that are preventing the team from performing at its best, or ideas and suggestions that can improve the way things are done. In other cases people may ask for advice or support. If you don't listen, all of this will be lost; and, as a result, the motivation of the team and its performance will be much lower than it could be.

"Listening" is not as easy as it sounds. To fully concentrate on what the other person is saying and to assure that you fully understand what they mean requires effort and practice.

Many people assume they know what someone means as soon as they have heard the first couple of sentences. How often have you heard someone say, "Oh yes, I know what you mean…" before you have had the chance to get your whole message across. Bear in mind that often the most important piece of information comes at the end. Do not interrupt.

	Question	usually	sometimes	seldom
1	I maintain eye contact with the speaker when listening.			
2	The speaker's appearance and the style and quality of his or her delivery greatly affect whether I think what is said is worthwhile.			
3	I try to align my thoughts and feelings with those of the speaker.			
4	I listen for specific facts rather than for the "big picture."			
5	I listen for both factual content and the emotion behind the literal words.			

How Did You Score?

Questions 2, 4, 9, 10		Questions 1, 3, 5, 6, 7, 8	
Usually	1 point	Usually	3 points
Sometimes	2 points	Sometimes	2 points
Seldom	3 points	Seldom	1 point

More than 27
Your listening skills seem to be good, but there may be room for improvement in some areas.

22–26
You have some skills, but you could use considerable improvement.

Under 22
Your skills need substantial improvement in many areas.

	Question	usually	sometimes	seldom
6	I ask questions for clarification.			
7	I withold judgement of what the speaker has said until he or she has finished.			
8	I make a conscious effort to evaluate the logic and consistency of what is being said.			
9	While listening, I think about what I am going to say as soon as I have my chance.			
10	I prefer to be the last person to speak.			

Discussing Problems And Getting Agreement

When discussing difficult subjects it is important that you do not lose sight of the core issues and the need to reach a resolution. There is a tendency in some organizations for team leaders to impose agreement on other people – "So, that's what we've agreed upon … right?" when, in fact, that is what the leader has just decided. This imposition of one person's view is counterproductive. Agreement means that everyone involved accepts the decision. It is probably not very often that a boss says to someone on his or her team, "It's not critical what I think; but it is critical what you think of this because you are going to be the one doing the job." Getting real agreement can be both difficult and time consuming, but the benefit is that you have everybody working at full potential towards the same goals, rather than half-heartedly towards different goals.

Attempts to coerce other people into doing what you want may end in short-term success, but it always results in long-term failure. Agreement should be reached by mutual consent, not by intimidation.

	Question	usually	sometimes	seldom
1	I state my position at once and then invite discussion.			
2	I always look for a mutually beneficial outcome.			
3	I never back away from a good argument.			
4	I help the other person understand how to solve the problem even if it takes time.			
5	I try to understand other people's views.			
6	People come to me with their problems.			

How Did You Score?

Questions 1, 3, 7, 9, 10, 12		Questions 2, 4, 5, 6, 8, 11	
Usually	1 point	Usually	3 points
Sometimes	2 points	Sometimes	2 points
Seldom	3 points	Seldom	1 point

More than 32
Your negotiating skills seem to be good, but there may be room for improvement in some areas.

26–32
You have some skills, but you could use considerable improvement.

Under 26
Your skills need substantial improvement in many areas.

	Question	usually	sometimes	seldom
7	I tell people what their problems are.			
8	I always stick to facts and events and never insult the other person.			
9	I am prepared to give in totally, rather than force someone else to change their mind.			
10	I always put any controversial issues to one side to avoid problems.			
11	I let the other person explain his or her position first.			
12	I let other people have their way if they start getting emotional.			

3

Getting it right
Basic principles
Preparation
Delivery

How does communication work?

How can I prepare my message?

Was my message understood?

How Communication Works

Communication has been successful if the message that is received is the same as the one sent. This simple model shows all of the factors that can affect the communication process. In the model the message is sent by a sender to a recipient (who could be either an individual or a group). Of course, the roles can switch during the course of a conversation as the receiver replies and becomes the sender. The model shows that communication can be complex.

Encoding and transmitting the message
Encoding is taking what you want to say and presenting it in a way the receiver will understand. You use the transmitters – the senses of hearing, seeing, touching – to communicate. Try listening to someone talking to you when your eyes are closed. This shows how much nonverbal signals contribute to understanding messages. Even if you say that you are interested, by looking bored or repeatedly checking your watch, you send other signals.

The message moves into the communication channels

Note the noise area between the sender and receiver that may impact upon the message. Noise can be any background distraction, such as workmen or someone talking. It can also be a distraction, which does not make an actual sound, such as something on your mind that affects your concentration. These are all things that can prevent another person from understanding the message as the sender intended. Remember the last conversation you tried to have next to a busy major road or in a noisy car, or think of the times when you have tried to have a telephone conversation at the same time as you were doing some paperwork. The noise probably made getting your message across much more difficult than it would normally have been. You need to minimize this noise by removing or reducing all distractions that may impair the ability of the recipient to focus on your message. It is not only the message that is important, but where and how it is delivered.

Arriving at the receptors

Other people's senses are important because they are the receptors that take in the message. Are they listening and watching? Are they paying attention? Are they tuned in to receiving a message? Are they listening for the critical parts of the message? Have you ever noticed that someone you are talking to is nodding as you speak but clearly not paying attention? You probably wonder whether that person is thinking about your message or what she will be doing over the weekend. Also, people with disabilities – who may have lost the use of sight, hearing, or other receptors – require special effort to be sure that they can understand your message. For example, someone who can't see very well will not pick up your nonverbal signals (your hand gestures and smile).

Decoding

Each person will decode the message according to his or her own perceptions, not those of the sender, and will interpret the message in a unique way. If there is a difference in perception, there will be confusion. Consider the potential problems when you are communicating with a large group. Have you ever been to a meeting at which you and other people have heard the same words, but later disagreed on what was actually said or what was meant by the words? As you prepare your message, try to consider the different ways that it could be interpreted by the people receiving it. For example, if your boss were to announce, "There are a lot of changes coming up," some people may see it as a threat, others as an opportunity.

Why on earth bother with this complex process?
How often have you heard at work *"Oh…that's what you meant; I thought you wanted me to …"* or, *"No, no, I didn't mean that… I meant this…"* Understanding the model allows you to make sure your message gets through and helps you avoid problems that may arise.

The First Steps To Effective Communication

Getting your message across is not as simple as it may sound at first. It is up to the sender to make sure that the recipient gets the message and that the message received matches the one that was sent. Many factors contribute to even the most simple forms of communication, and many problems can arise. If the message does not get through, it is probably the fault of the sender. For example, if the person at the other end forgets to switch on his or her fax machine, it is still the sender's fault if the message does not get through, because the sender should have checked by telephone that the fax has arrived.

How the message is worded has a great impact on how it is received and understood. For example, "Write out the sales figures NOW !" or "Peter, would you please write out the latest sales figures for me?" say different things.

The content of the message is crucial. Consider whether the message in the example conveys everything necessary. Does Peter write out the sales figures by area or by product? Does he write them in ascending or descending order, and should he use some kind of graphics?

The means by which the message is delivered – face to face, on the telephone, or as a memo – will also affect the way the message is received. Evidence suggests that in most communication, particularly verbal, the first delivery of a message is usually only 50 percent successful, so there is plenty of room for improvement. Written communication has the advantage of being open to less misinterpretation. Yet, how many times have you "skim read" a document and not really understood the message it contains, got the wrong message, or had to reread or seek further clarification?

Perception and understanding

All too often we assume that other people share our experiences, perceptions, and views. Unfortunately this is not the case, and the perceptions of the audience will affect the way it is interpreted. To communicate effectively it is important that the receiver understands your perceptions about a message, as well as the message itself. If someone likes you, he or she will take the message seriously. If not, they may

THE STAGES OF EFFECTIVE COMMUNICATION

- You construct the message.
- You match the message to the recipient.
- You prepare the receiver.
- You send the message.
- They receive the message.
- They interpret the message.
- You confirm the message has been understood.

EXERCISE

Sometimes, even though we have given the right information, the other person still misunderstands. Who is at fault? Describe a swing hanging from a tree branch to another person. Do not use the word "swing" and not mention what a swing is designed to do. Ask the other person to draw what you are describing. It is unlikely that the finished picture will look like the swing you had in your imagination.

ignore it! The recipient may not view the matter in the same way you do. You may think doing the sales figures is an important job; someone else may think it is tedious. It is important that the receiver understands your perception. Take note of the difference between your perception and hers and draw attention to it. You might say, "I know you don't think preparing the sales figures is important, but it is essential that it is done for my team to be able to operate effectively. We think it's very important."

Everyone is different

Quickly jot down the swing you were describing in the exercise on the previous page. Is this the only way it could be imagined? Ask a couple of people to do the same exercise, and compare their pictures with yours and the illustrations (right). No doubt they all look at least slightly different. Each of us has unique associations and experiences, which determine exactly how we think about things – even something as simple as a swing in a tree.

This has implications for the message and how it is delivered. Explain your perceptions as part of the message to avoid confusion. Do not assume that the other person will "catch your drift."

There are three stages in sending a successful message

1 preparation

2 delivery

3 confirmation of understanding

It is often said that many drafts end up becoming the final message. Allow yourself enough time to structure and target your message, so that it is in a form that will make it easy for the recipient to understand. Some messages will not take long to fine tune to match the receiver, especially if you are giving a simple message to someone who you know. Others need careful preparation, e.g., if you are giving a long message to a group of your superiors. In such cases, allow yourself plenty of time to prepare your message.

Preparing The Message

I keep six honest serving
men. They taught me all
I knew. Their names are
What and Why and
When, and How and
Where and Who

Rudyard Kipling

Careful construction of the message, as well as matching its form and delivery to the audience is critical for success. Do not neglect this stage of communication. Good preparation will assure that the delivery goes smoothly. It will also help you avoid any barriers to your message as a result of someone who is not prepared to receive it or an incomplete or inaccurate message that does not match the person for whom it was intended. Whether you are preparing a study on a complex subject or a quick briefing for a simple task, the principles are the same.

Constructing the initial message

Put together the message you want to send, so that you achieve your objective. The first question is, "What do I want to achieve?" For example, is it to get a specific job done, to brief a group on the plans for next year, or to talk over performance problems with a team member?

The message itself can be structured with the help of Rudyard Kipling's poem *Six Honest Serving Men* (left), a poem everyone who plans anything should know. Try to memorize it if you can. It will prove very useful in any number of situations.

Using this format ensures that all of the critical information is included. The structure is simple: ask youself what you want to achieve, why it needs to be done, when it needs to be done by, how it can best be achieved, where it needs to happen, and who needs to do it. This method is illustrated by the examples on the opposite page, where it has been used to plan some typical work messages.

Hopefully, your version, based on the suggested format, was similar. You may need to add more detail if the receiver needs it. It may be useful to give details on what the problems were. Read what you have written, and think about whether your version would have communicated your message successfully.

TELLING YOUR TEAM ABOUT THE NEW PRODUCTS BEING LAUNCHED

You can apply the format suggested by the poem to constructing a message:

WHAT do I want to achieve? **I want to inform the team about the new products.**

WHY should it be done? **Because they need to know what is coming up so they will be able to answer client questions when the products are launched.**

WHEN does it need to be completed? **They should be made aware immediately and become fully conversant by January of next year.**

HOW should it be done? **They have preliminary knowledge now and will need to read spec sheets which are due out next month.**

WHERE? **There will be an initial presentation in the training room. Then, they should do the rest of their preparation on their own time, outside work.**

WHO by? **All team members must be totally familiar with all new products.**

SO WHAT IS THE FINAL MESSAGE ?

"You all need to know about these new products so that you can answer client questions. I'm letting you know now to give you time to read up on them and become experts by next January. The spec sheets will be out next month."

YOU HAVE TO DISCUSS A PERFORMANCE PROBLEM WITH KATHERINE, ONE OF YOUR TEAM

You can apply the same format to constructing a message for one-to-one communications:

WHAT DO I NEED TO ACHIEVE? **An improvement in Katherine's performance.**

WHY DOES IT NEED TO BE DONE? **Because her performance is not as good as I need for the team to be effective. There are problems with her technical skills.**

WHEN DOES IT NEED TO BE DONE BY? **As soon as possible.**

HOW IS IT BEST DONE? **By agreeing steps and targets to improve her performance.**

WHERE? **At work and possibly with the help of a training course.**

WHO by? **A partnership between her and me.**

SO WHAT IS THE FINAL MESSAGE ?

Write down what you think the message would be then compare it to the suggested one below:

"Katherine, you need to improve some of your technical skills to allow the team to be effective. We need to do this as soon as possible and we will agree steps and targets in partnership to achieve this, possibly sending you on a training course."

Matching The Message To The Receiver

Once you have decided what you want to say, the next step is to fine tune your message to match the audience. Each message you send has to be tailored to the recipient. For example, you would not talk to a group of your colleagues in the same way you would to a group of 11 year olds. You need to think about exactly how you will get your message across to the audience. Which words will you use? Are technical words suitable? Does your audience already sympathize with your viewpoint, or do you have to convince them?

Do you have to get the message over to one of your team, the board of your organization, a colleague in an office on the other side of the world, or a group of strangers with whom you have never met? Even within your own team, there may be a difference in the way you would communicate your message.

The two areas you should think about carefully as you try to match the message to the audience are information and delivery style.

Information Try to match the level of information in the message to the needs of the person receiving it. The amount of detail depends on how much this person already knows about the subject. There is an important link to delegation if the message is a request to do something on your behalf.

Compare how you would get the same job done by a senior, experienced colleague with the way you would brief an inexperienced trainee? The objective – getting the job done – is the same, but you would need to include more information for the inexperienced trainee. He or she would need to be told not only how to do the job but also why it needs to be done. The more experienced colleague would know this information already.

Delivery style Do you take a quiet step-by-step approach – checking the other person's understanding at each stage? Or, do you deliver the message fast and furiously? Do you use many practical examples, or concentrate on the theory?

When you speak, try to achieve a clear, friendly tone that is matched to the listener. Again, you can probably think of individuals you work with to whom you would deliver the same message in different ways.

To help match the message to the listener, these are some of the questions you may want to ask yourself. Although the questions in the chart below refer to "them," this matching process is just as important with individuals as with groups. *All* of these questions apply equally to communication with individuals and groups.

Who is receiving the message?	What is their perception of you?
Why are they there?	What do they want from you?
	What do you want from them?
What do they know about the subject?	Will this limit the use of technical words?
	Will they understand the concepts?
	Will they know if you get things wrong?
	Are they more expert, less expert, or on the same level as you?
What is their link to you?	Are they superiors, members of your team, peers, or people you've not met before?
Are they on your side, or do you have to win them over?	
Are there those who will have difficulty with technical phrases?	
Are there non-English speakers?	What is their level of English?
	Will this limit the words you can use?
	Will you need to learn the key phrases in another language?
How big is the audience?	The larger the audience, the more impersonal the communication process becomes and the more important it is to "get them on your side." This is especially true if they don't know you.
How formal is the message?	Some messages, such as presentations to superiors, are very formal.

Deciding On The Means Of Delivery

Think about written information sources you use at work, such as handbooks. Their advantage is that you can dip into them at the place and time you want. But remember written messages can be lost!

You can deliver your message either verbally or in writing. Verbal delivery includes presentations, one to one, team meetings, and telephone. Written delivery includes letters, reports, e-mails, or memos. Select the one that gets the message across as effectively as possible and maximizes the listener's ability to understand it as you intended. But bear in mind that the method you use to communicate will send a secondary message, such as, "If he thought it was really that important, he should have put it in writing," or, "She could have spoken to me about it, rather than sending me an e-mail." Do not forget this aspect of message sending.

Delivery mechanics This addresses the means of delivering the message from the purely technical perspective. If the message is complex and difficult for the other person to remember, or will require taking voluminous notes, a written message may be more effective.

WHEN TRYING TO DECIDE WHICH METHOD OF DELIVERY IS BEST SUITED TO A PARTICULAR SITUATION, ASK YOURSELF THE FOLLOWING QUESTIONS:

1 Do I need a record of what happened?

2 Is the volume/complexity of information so great that the receiver will be unable to take it in all at one time?

3 Do I want the receiver to be able to respond at once to my message?

4 Do I want the receiver to be able to think about the message and respond at a later date?

5 How many people do I want to get the message? Is it the same message for all of them?

6 Do I want to be able to change, add to, or fine tune the message as I deliver it?

7 Is it a formal or informal message?

8 Am I unable to contact the receiver verbally, or is it very difficult to do so?

9 Are there geographical or physical restrictions on the means I can use?

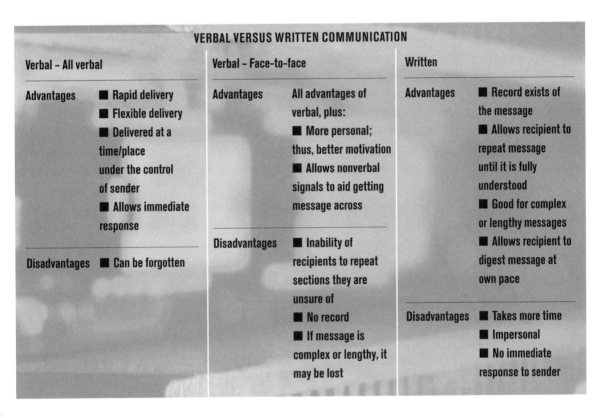

VERBAL VERSUS WRITTEN COMMUNICATION

Verbal – All verbal		Verbal – Face-to-face		Written	
Advantages	■ Rapid delivery ■ Flexible delivery ■ Delivered at a time/place under the control of sender ■ Allows immediate response	Advantages	All advantages of verbal, plus: ■ More personal; thus, better motivation ■ Allows nonverbal signals to aid getting message across	Advantages	■ Record exists of the message ■ Allows recipient to repeat message until it is fully understood ■ Good for complex or lengthy messages ■ Allows recipient to digest message at own pace
Disadvantages	■ Can be forgotten	Disadvantages	■ Inability of recipients to repeat sections they are unsure of ■ No record ■ If message is complex or lengthy, it may be lost	Disadvantages	■ Takes more time ■ Impersonal ■ No immediate response to sender

Written messages also provide a record of the content and allow the receiver to refer back to the original wording, as well as digest the information at their own speed over a period of time. This is crucial if you expect a response from your audience, who needs time to think and consider.

Verbal messages are more personal, especially when delivered face to face. They allow immediate response and faster development of ideas or solutions than written ones. Verbal messages are more effective for quickly communicating simple messages, but they can also be easily forgotten.

In some circumstances, both verbal and written messages are necessary. For example, when ordering office supplies you may want to make a telephone call and follow it up with a faxed confirmation. A verbal account of a forthcoming meeting may need to be followed by a written agenda. The written message will reinforce the verbal message, enhancing the perception of the message's priority in the eyes of the person receiving it.

Getting The Delivery Right

The most obvious choice of a mechanical delivery method won't necessarily make the best impression. For example, your annual performance appraisal could be faxed to you quickly and effectively, but what would you think of this means of delivery? You would probably feel that this is the sort of matter that really should be dealt with face to face. If a message is to have a personal impact on the recipient, it should be delivered verbally – preferably face to face – and, if that is not possible, on the telephone.

The message is more than the words

The nonverbal signals you send with your body language in face to face communication also send a message. For example, a smile will help the recipient feel relaxed. Try to lean towards the other person during the conversation and maintain eye contact. This will create confidence that you are sincere in what you are saying.

If you are receiving a message, you can also accidentally give off the wrong signals. For example, if you look around the room, while someone is talking to you, this could easily be interpreted as boredom on your part.

Rehearse the delivery

Because you want to get the message right, you should practice it when possible. This is particularly important if the message is to be delivered face to face. While it may seem obvious that you would practice before addressing a group, surely there is no need to rehearse a one-on-one encounter. But why shouldn't you? If the message is important, you may find that if you say it as you first intended, it may not sound right. Try to get another person to listen to you as you practice. This may give you another perspective on how it sounds or how it could be misunderstood.

If your message is in writing, it may seem impossible to practice your delivery, but reading it through is good practice. Check to be sure the message makes sense, even if you have to read the letter or memo to yourself. In haste, you may find that you use the wrong words or fail to get the message right. Again, you may find that letting another person check over what you have written is a wise precaution. It is easy to miss your own mistakes in a written document because your brain will automatically "correct" them as you read. However, this still leaves the mistakes on the paper.

Doing The Support Work

You have now prepared your message and practiced giving it, so all you have to do now is deliver it. But where and when? Are you prepared, in case the other person asks questions? Do you have all the equipment you need? Are the correct resources in place to ensure an effective delivery of your message? This is particularly important if you have a formal message to convey, but it also applies to informal, day-to-day communication.

Plan to deliver the message at an appropriate time and in an appropriate place. If you need to get an important message across, make an appointment; and, if necessary, put it in your daily planner. This will avoid interruptions during the meeting. Also, by planning an appropriate time and place, you will be better able to prepare what you are going to say, you will be more relaxed, and the whole tone of the message will improve. This will reduce distraction and noise that may blunt your message. For example, it would be better to discuss an employee's poor performance in a private room, rather than in the main office where everyone can hear. Consider whether you will have to set a time in advance to talk in private.

If you are giving a presentation or chairing a meeting, check to be sure that any equipment you need – seating, a chart, an overhead projector, or refreshments – are there and that everything works. There is nothing quite as embarassing as turning on the overhead projector at a critical point in a meeting only to find out that it doesn't work. It also disrupts the flow of the meeting and undermines your message.

Make sure you have read everything you need to and that all necessary paperwork has been completed. Bring any handouts or reference material with you, as well as paper and a pen if you will need to make notes as you go along.

If you have to read from notes, the message is probably a complicated one; and your audience may wish to take notes on what is said. If you haven't informed people beforehand to bring a pen and paper, you should provide them. There is no point in clearly explaining a complex message if it is later forgotten. You can make sure that everyone has all of the critical information by providing pre-prepared notes. These can include background information, which is not covered in your message, but which may be of value to the audience.

The more important the communication, the more time you should allow to verify it.

Doing The Support Work

SUPPORT CHECKLIST

1 Venue

Choose where you intend to deliver the message. Will you need to make arrangements?
Do you need to tell the recipient?

2 Equipment

Do you need overheads, handouts, or other equipment to help you get the message across?
Will others need to take notes?
Will you serve refreshments?

3 Timing

How long will you need to convey your message? When will you do it?
This applies not only to presenting to a large audience, but also to most other forms of
communication. Have you made sure you that you will not be disturbed?

4 Paperwork

Have you read all of the related papers? Do you have all the supporting documents?
Will you need to take notes?

5 Yourself

In addition to checking your resources, it is worth making sure that your preliminary
preparation is thorough. Arriving late and looking untidy sends a message to the other
person: you can't be bothered, or you can't organize yourself to arrive on time. How
important is your message? Any rush, confusion, or stress will distract you from getting
your message across in the best possible way.
Try to arrive five minutes early to be sure that everything is in place and to relax.

Preparing The Receiver

Ensure that the audience is going to give its full attention to your message. If it is important, provide plenty of advance warning that you are about to deliver the message. In most day-to-day communication, preparation for a message usually takes place immediately before the message is delivered. For example, you might say, "John, could I please have a word with you about…" or "I think this is an important issue that we need to discuss." But, in some cases, such as team briefings, meetings, complex discussions, and appraisals, more warning is needed. This is especially important if you expect the other person to respond in detail to any of your points or questions. He or she will need time to prepare properly before the meeting.

If a team meeting is scheduled, alert the team verbally; and then confirm the time, date, and location in writing. If you want to discuss something with an individual, inform him or her beforehand. In many cases, the communication may also need a response from the other person. Advance warning provides important time to put together one's responses or thoughts, or to gather necessary information. If both sender and receiver have prepared themselves in advance of the meeting, both will get much more benefit from the communication.

SUMMARY
Using the "What, why, when, where, how, and who" format can make the whole preparation process easier. Consider the case study on page 37, *Telling the team about new products being launched.* This is how the message could have been planned using Kipling's poem.

I want to tell the team about the new products within the next week in a face to face meeting with discussion. That will require a room with an overhead projector. It will probably take 90 minutes, and I will supply handouts about the new products at the end. I may need someone from the production team to answer any technical questions that come up, so I must contact them in advance.

The preparation phase has now put the foundation in place to ensure that the delivery of your message goes smoothly. If you have done your preparation correctly, the actual delivery will probably go without any problems.

Delivering Your Message

If your boss says, "You are the most professional person I have ever worked with," in a genuine way, it can boost your confidence greatly. But if it is said sarcastically, it can destroy your confidence. Though the same words are used, the meaning is exactly opposite. So, think carefully about your tone of voice, and be sure it supports what you want to say.

Getting the message receiver's attention and giving notice of your intention to communicate well in advance may be appropriate for some situations such as meetings, but for most day-to-day communications – such as answering a question – this can be done immediately before you deliver your message. For example, you might say, "Here is the answer to your question, John. Sales fell by 20 percent last month."

Prepare the other person for the main message by following five steps outlined below. This method can be applied in a range of situations, from giving a presentation to a large number of people to passing on a piece of information on the telephone. The preparation sets the stage for the main message so that the receiver is ready and willing to receive it.

1 **Determine if the audience is ready to receive the message and to give feedback.** Even though the recipient(s) are present, be certain they are ready to receive your message. Even if you have assured that the time and place are appropriate for the delivery of the message, there are other immediate distractions that may prevent successful communication. Therefore, double check that the receiver is relaxed and listening for your message.

2 **Outline what the message is about.** Set the scene. It is useful to provide a brief outline of what you intend to cover in your message. This outline has exactly the same function as the executive summary in a report or the introduction to a presentation.

3 **Background** Put the communication in the proper context. Explain the background. For example, tell your assistant that you want him to pay attention to the presentation of his report because there has recently been a memo to all managers about badly presented work.

4 **Explain why the information is important to you.** This is confirmation of your assumptions and perceptions. It establishes why you are sending the message and your thoughts or attitudes about it. This ensures that others interpret the message from your perspective. They may disagree with your viewpoint; but, at least, they will understand what it is. Many people forget the importance of this. If the message doesn't include how you view the issue – as important or urgent, for example – others may not respond as you wish. Communicating your perception is critical.

5 **Explain how the information will benefit the listener.** In any communication, there needs to be some compelling reason to accept the message. You should try to bear this in mind. Think about when to assign a task or job to members of your team. If you point out how the job will benefit them – for example, by enabling them to gain experience or by learning more about a certain area – this improves their motivation, both to listen to the message and to do the job.

Delivering the message Now that you have decided on the most effective approach to delivery, you will want to deliver your message to the absolute best of your ability.

If you have chosen to verbally deliver your message, be sure to use an appropriate tone and body language to back up your message. These factors are just as important as the words you use. Keep eye contact, and speak clearly, with a confident and friendly tone. Speak up, be direct, be specific. Avoid "ummm" and "er," and cut out any unnecessary detail or waffling. If it is appropriate, smile as you speak to put the receiver at ease. Be sincere. Do not talk too fast, and check that the audience is keeping up. If the message is verbal, watch and listen to see that the audience appears to be taking it in. Is it acknowledging your points? Agreeing with you? Showing interest? With a telephone message, you have to listen for these signals. If you feel that your audience may be getting confused, stop and ask if they understand. Rephrase the point if necessary. The more complex the message, the more often you should check for understanding. Usually, you are building up to a conclusion that contains the critical part of the message, so it is essential that others have clearly understood the logical progression of ideas and thoughts.

Do not forget that getting feedback can apply to situations where people may be more experienced or knowledgeable than you. They can give you information or advice that will help you do your job better. "What do you think of this proposal?" can get valuable feedback for you and, at the same time, show your respect for the individual.

Has Your Message Been Understood?

People do not use the feedback loop because:
- **they think that, because they understand their own message, everyone else will too**
- **they don't have time to check for understanding**
- **they do not want to suggest that the other person was not listening**

This feedback stage is the most frequently overlooked part of the communication process, yet it is of critical importance. It is your last chance to check that the message has been understood before things start to happen or, potentially, go wrong. This is true, not only if you have asked people to do things, but also if you have given them information. Their views, opinions, and plans are being formed the moment you stop communicating. If you do not check for understanding and acceptance of your message, those views, opinions, and plans may not be what you intended to convey.

To ensure that your message was understood as you intended, solicit feedback from the receiver by asking questions and listening to the answers.

The very least you should do is to ask if there are any questions, then use both active listening *and* questioning as often as possible to be sure that your message was received as you planned.

In the basic communication model on page 32, the "feedback loop" is where the sender asks the receiver to confirm the message, in order to see if it matches the message sent. However, simply asking "do you understand" may not always tell you if there has been genuine understanding. People tend to say what they think others want to hear, especially at work, because they are afraid that admitting that they do not understand may make them appear stupid. Also, people may think they have understood what you meant, but actually totally misunderstood your point. So ask the other person to tell you what they think your message is. Be sure to ask questions, but do not forget to listen to the answers. If the message is anything other than very simple, you may find it more effective to work in stages; after each important point, confirm that the message has been understood.

With written messages, we all assume recipients will come back to us if they are unsure or unhappy, but this often doesn't happen. If you have sent a written message, you should also verbally check that it has been understood, just as you would in conversation. Try to do this whenever possible to see if the receiver raises any concerns. Because it has been put in writing, he or she may feel that you are not interested in their view.

MOST CLOSED QUESTIONS CAN BE QUITE EASILY TURNED INTO OPEN QUESTIONS

Closed question – "Do you think this plan is ok?"

Open question – "What problems do you feel might occur if we use this plan?"

Questions This is always important, not just when you want to send a message and check understanding, but at any time you need to check what other people think. Use questions in all situations to check how effective your communication has been. To ascertain whether your message was clear, just ask the audience what it thought you were trying to say.

Asking open questions (questions that don't have a "yes" or "no" answer) is a good way to get a response from someone who is reluctant to give feedback. Open questions usually start with the words "how, what, when, where, why," which often encourage a response and cannot generally be answered with a simple one-word reply. Open questions make the receipients give you more feedback than just "yes" or "no," which helps you decide whether they have really understood.

Active listening If you ask a question, listen to the answer. All of it. Allow the other person time to compose an answer and to deliver it fully before you speak again. Do not interrupt them.

As you listen, try to support the person who is talking, confirming that you understand by nodding as he or she speaks. If you sense difficulty, try to help the person phrase the reply; but check with him or her as you do this. For example, you might ask, "So, are you telling me you are not very happy with the new holiday timetable for the Christmas break?"

At the end of a response to a question, confirm that you have correctly understood what has been said by paraphrasing and asking for confirmation that you have received and understood the message correctly. For more details on active listening, see page 59.

Write down three recent times when something went wrong at work. At which stage do you think the problem occurred? For example, did the initial message leave out vital information you needed, or was the failure one of interpretation? For each case, jot down a few notes about how the problem could have been avoided. This will enable you to identify some of the barriers to communication that can occur.

Barriers To Communications

Barriers that prevent your message from getting through can have disastrous results. For example, if a faulty telephone line resulted in clients being unable to get through when they needed to, valuable sales might be lost. Watch out for barriers that could prevent your message getting through each time you communicate. Some of the barriers may be your fault, some the fault of technology, but they are rarely the fault of the person who is receiving the message. Barriers can arise at each stage of the communication process.

	Stage	Barrier	Example	Solution
1	Constructing the message	The message was incomplete.	You forgot to give the deadline for a piece of work.	Be sure the message contains all the information needed and accurately reflects what you mean.
		The message was inaccurate; you did not express what you really meant.	You said that you would like to have "a chat some time soon," when you really wanted "an urgent meeting."	
2	Matching the message	The message was not "tuned in" to those who were to receive it. This applies just as much to communicating with one person as to a group.	You used too many technical words for a non-technical audience. You used a tone that was unsympathetic to the audience. You spoke too fast.	Be sure the message is matched to the recipient by adjusting the level of information, as well as your style and tone. Add information about your perceptions if the receiver's perceptions are likely to be different.
3	Preparing the recipient	The recipient was not ready to accept the message.	The recipient was not expecting a message; they were busy with another task and were not paying attention.	Be sure the message is delivered away from distractions and that the other person is ready to receive it before you begin.

	Stage	Barrier	Example	Solution
4	Sending the message	The means by which the message was sent was inappropriate.	A long and complicated fax could have been replaced effectively by a five-minute face to face briefing.	Make sure the means of delivery is appropriate to the message. Ask yourself if you would like to have this message delivered to you in this way?
5	Receiving the message	There was some problem in the arrival of the message.	The receiver was out sick for a day and missed the message. The e-mail was delayed by a computer failure.	Ensure that the means of delivery will get the message to the right place at the right time. If necessary confirm the delivery – things can go missing. When communicating face to face minimize distractions.
6	Interpreting the message	The message was not understood as intended.	You did not tell the other person that something was important because you thought it was obvious. The recipient had a different idea of what was important.	Try to understand the perceptions and assumptions of the receiver. Feed this into the "matching the message" process and include information on your perceptions.
7	Confirming the message	You failed to seek or listen to feedback; there was no confirmation of the message being correctly received.	You did not check for understanding and as a result the receiver did not get the job done on time.	Always check the message the receiver has received via feedback – using questions and listening. This is your last chance to make sure your message has got across as you intended before things start to happen.

4

Face to face

Telephone

Feedback

Written word

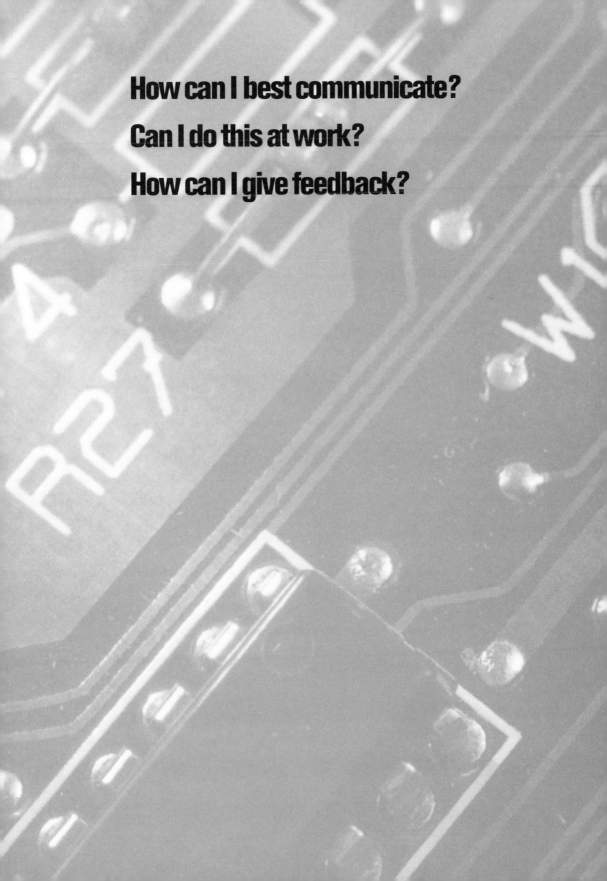

How can I best communicate?

Can I do this at work?

How can I give feedback?

Getting It Right At Work

It's wise to build on your current skills. This chapter looks at the situations that come up most often at work and provides you with strategies you can use immediately to make your communication more effective. The main areas covered are one-to-one communication, group meetings, written communication, and telephone communication.

Face to face with another person

Discussing an issue face to face can save time. A meeting allows you to communicate complex ideas. A one-to-one situation means that you are on the spot, ready to deal with any questions and problems then and there. This type of communication can also have a great motivational effect on your team members. You have the opportunity to fully involve other people in the subject under discussion. This means that all those involved fully understand what they need to do and why.

By talking to people face to face, you will also be able to maintain the initiative. You will be able to anticipate and dispel rumors and hearsay before they begin. Although sometimes it may be tempting to allow things to drift, remember that it is better for people to be kept informed about developments and decisions, even if they are not happy about them.

Prepare yourself well before you talk to someone face to face. Before you begin be sure that you have clarified the following points in your own mind:

- What is the message about?
- What is the background to the message?
- Why is it important to you?
- Why is it important to the recipient?
- Why is it important to the company?
- How will the message be of benefit to the person who receives it?

KEEP IMPROVING
In the wide variety of situations you may face at work, there is no simple answer to getting it right. Keep referring back to the basic format of communication. It will guide you through a logical process to produce the right message and deliver it effectively. Then "fine tune" your methods, using the following sections, which cover the main areas of communication encountered in the work place.

CASE STUDY

You would like John to take charge of opening a new branch office in Paris.
He has the management skills and experience, and he speaks fluent French.

WHAT DO I WANT TO ACHIEVE? **To convince John to open and run the new Paris office.**

WHY SHOULD IT BE DONE? **The Paris office has to open and he is the best candidate.**

WHEN SHOULD IT OCCUR? **The office must be open by next October.**

HOW IS IT BEST DONE? **By releasing John from his current post in three months in order to concentrate on preparing for the Paris opening.**

WHERE? **London and Paris.**

WHO? **John and some administrative support.**

Note down the message components:

 John to run the new Paris office
 Best candidate
 Opening on October 1 next year
 He can be released to start in Paris in three months
 Based London/Paris
 Administrative support will be provided.
 Ask for confirmation, and get feedback.

The final message is:

"John, as you know, there is to be a new office in Paris at the end of next year. This will be a first step in our expansion into Europe so it is very important that it is successful. Because of your experience and fluent French I'd like you to run it. This is obviously a very good opportunity for you to advance your career and help develop the company. You could start work in three months and will get administrative support. What are your views on this offer?"

Face to Face With A Group

Many managers shy away from speaking to their team as a group, although they are happy to speak to them as individuals! Do you prefer to deal with people individually, even if the information you want to convey is common to all of them? Do you try to avoid a meeting by putting up a notice on the bulletin board? Though putting up a notice gets your message across, it is only effective for the most simple messages. If there is any chance that the people concerned want to ask questions or seek further explanation, it is not effective.

This type of communication involves talking to the people you work with on a daily basis. However, it can also apply to giving a presentation or speaking to a group of strangers. The principles are the same. Speaking face to face with a group is easier and more efficient than giving the same information to everyone individually. It also ensures that everyone gets the same message at the same time. Face to face communication has the one big advantage of allowing others to respond immediately.

The general principles of conducting briefings and team meetings are covered in this section. Formal presentations are not dealt with specifically here, but the same principles apply to speaking to any group of people.

Briefing the team When giving instructions to a team or an individual, many managers often leave out critical information. By following the format below you will ensure that all of the important information is included in your message. Before the start of the briefing, review all of the necessary preliminary preparations to make sure there are no technical problems.

BRIEFING THE TEAM	
Background	Tell the team why the task is necessary.
Objectives	Outline what the team or group is aiming to achieve.
General tasks	Let the team know the overall plan.
Specific tasks	Detail the objectives, stages, and individual tasks involved.
Administration	Tell everyone where support, resources, interim reports, action on problems, and contacts are coming from.
Timing	Outline the start time, finish, and intermediate stages or deadlines.
Any questions?	Don't forget the crucial feedback stage.

Team meetings Meetings may be called regularly or on an ad-hoc basis to deal with particular situations. Expect more team involvement and that a number of messages may need to be presented and discussed. The structure of the meeting must allow for discussion. Getting your team meetings to run smoothly is very important. Badly run team meetings are one of the most common sources of wasted time in organizations.

The following format should help your meetings run well and get your message across, resulting in improved team motivation.

Leading the meeting In some cases the team meeting is an opportunity for you to provide information, such as explaining plans for the future. Alternatively, a meeting may be used to gather information, for example, if a group of employees wants you to pass on some ideas or concerns to the boss.

As a group leader, it is your job to give everyone the opportunity to get their message across.

In your organization, there may be no formal system for regular team meetings; but you can run them for your team.

TEAM MEETINGS

Set the stage.	Give advance notice of time and place. Do your preliminary preparation.
Prepare the message.	Group the points you wish to make. Make the information relevant to the audience. Review the team's performance (if applicable). Try to anticipate any questions.
Get their attention.	Tell everyone what the meeting is about. Outline the background of the subject under discussion. Explain why the message is important to you, them, and the organization. Explain how they will benefit.
Deliver the message.	Explain your message, the problem, or matter to be discussed.
Ask for feedback.	Let the team members contribute their views.
Control the meeting.	Don't allow side discussions. Allow only one person to talk at once. If you ask for input, get it from everyone. Avoid distractions. Support your boss.
Summarize.	Sum up what has been agreed upon. Detail what is to be done, by whom and when. Plan for the next meeting.

Follow up – After the meeting a written version of your summary will ensure that what has been agreed, what is to be done, by who and by when is available to all. This will ensure that it gets done.

Getting Effective Feedback

FEEDBACK:

■ Gives us more information for decision making

■ Gives us better information for decision making

■ Assures that information or instructions have been understood or actioned

■ Allows staff to solve problems that are restricting their performance

■ Facilitates management learning

■ May increase employee satisfaction, motivation, and performance

If you have to plan or organize anything, two-way communication is vital to ensuring that it gets done correctly and in the best way possible. If you are to run a successful team, it is vital that your team gives you feedback. You need to be kept informed about how the task is going, how things could be made to work better, and how you are performing. Encouraging two-way communication is really a case of building trust. If your team trusts you, it will communicate openly and often, which will enable you to do your job more effectively. "What are your views on this?" can be one of the most effective ways of eliciting excellent ideas and improving the motivation of the person whose opinion you solicit. Many of us have found ourselves in the situation of having information or ideas that would help our team or organization or that we simply wanted to express, but some barrier prevented us sharing our ideas. These barriers must be removed for communication to work. Most are under your control, especially if you are a team leader. Roughly half your time should be spent listening. To get maximum value when someone offers feedback, use the skill of active listening, and always ask open questions.

MAJOR BARRIERS AGAINST FEEDBACK

■ The boss didn't want feedback or was unapproachable.

■ The boss never seems to listen to anything that is said.

■ No one asks for feedback.

■ Staff members felt that they were too junior or inexperienced or that their ideas would not be taken seriously.

■ There was no opportunity to give the feedback.

■ Fear of disagreeing with the boss was a factor.

If nothing is done to break down these barriers, the team will waste time and resources and, ultimately, become demotivated.

ACTIVE LISTENING

■ Find somewhere to talk where you will not be interrupted.

■ Show interest in the person who wishes to talk.

■ Listen until he or she has finished. The last few words are often the most important.

■ Pay attention physically; nod, smile, maintain eye contact.

■ Show support in your response and actions.

■ Check back to ensure you have understood exactly what the sender meant to say.

■ Help the sender structure his or her ideas if necessary.

■ Summarize, and agree on main points before moving on.

■ Build on the sender's argument. Don't substitute your own ideas.

■ Try to understand the other person's position.

■ Pay attention to what the speaker is NOT saying. This can be important as well.

■ Don't let your personal views interfere with the listening.

■ Relax, you listen better when relaxed.

To improve the amount and quality of feedback you receive, ask for feedback, listen to it. Act on it, if appropriate. Then let the person who provided you with information or an idea know what is being done about it.

■ Actively encourage feedback by asking for it.

■ Use active-listening skills.

■ Act on feedback; do something about it; give feedback on it.

■ Tell people what is happening as a result of their feedback.

■ Hold regular, two-way briefing sessions.

■ Build a team culture that encourages two-way communication.

It is the team leader's responsibility to ensure that he or she receives enough good quality feedback. When people are asked the main reason for not telling their boss what was going wrong or what they thought could be improved, most reply that their boss did not seem interested in their input. This is unforgivable and probably ruins any chance of getting the team to work well. They also say that no one asked for their opinion.

Giving Feedback To Others

Those who work for you need feedback on a day-to-day basis, as well as at their formal appraisals. One of the major criticisms of team leaders is often that they do not tell the people working for them where they stand. Saving up all of your information for the appraisal tries to address too many issues at once, making them harder to manage. Regular feedback on a day-to-day basis lets people know where they stand allows them to develop and improve their skills, and permits improvements to begin at once. Giving effective feedback is a critical part of task supervision and evaluation. It is also a major contributory factor to producing good team and individual motivation.

However, approaching feedback in the wrong way can demotivate the individual concerned. Everyone is sensitive to the discussion of personal performance.

Giving praise Some managers praise too little; some praise too often. The balance also varies according to who is being praised. Some individuals would not wish to be praised publicly; some would find just a word of thanks enough, while others would prefer time off. Try to get to know what motivates individuals on your team. A good motivator uses praise only when it has been earned. Praising just to create a pleasant atmosphere is a waste of time and makes people think they are doing well when they are not.

THE FOLLOWING GUIDELINES WILL HELP YOU TO GET IT RIGHT

■ Pick an appropriate time and place.
■ Be specific; both positive and negative feedback are more valuable when specific examples are given.
■ Give feedback in a logical sequence.
    – Measurable performance and facts
    – What this says about the individual
    – Consequences for the team or organization
    – Any resulting actions that may follow
■ Check that the person you are speaking to understands what you have said, ask questions and listen to the answers.
■ Give the other person an opportunity to contribute.
■ Try to take a positive approach. Even negative feedback should be geared to helping the individual improve his or her performance. For example, suggest how things can get better, and give examples of recent improvements. Constructive criticism, not censure, is required.

WHEN GIVING PRAISE, TRY TO STRESS THE FOLLOWING:

■ What was good about what the person or team did
■ Why was it good
■ What it says about them
■ The impact on the team or organization

perform as well as required boil down to one of the following:

■ not being told clearly what to do and not being checked for understanding
■ being given a task outside of their capabilities
■ not being given sufficient resources to do the job including time

Remember that rewards are more effective if people know in advance how they will benefit from good performance. Expectations and targets should be agreed upon by all the parties.

Targets should be within the abilities of the individuals concerned. People may be tempted to agree to do too much if you ask them, so try not to let this happen. If you set targets too high, people will never achieve them and, as a result, will become demotivated. The target should be realistic and challenging to allow the individual or team a good chance of success and praise, but difficult enough to develop and challenge them.

Giving negative feedback

Before you even consider giving negative feedback, you must be certain it is deserved. In all too many cases people are given negative feedback they really don't deserve. In the majority of cases the reasons an individual does not

All of these problems are the fault of the person delegating the job, not the person doing it. It may be a genuine misunderstanding. Perhaps you thought that they had the skills required, but did you check? There is nothing more likely to sour relationships with team members than accusing them of under-performing, when most of the fault lies with you as a manager. If you are sure that the problem lies with someone else, then deliver your message carefully.

Of all areas of communication, perhaps the most difficult is giving negative feedback. If the recipient becomes defensive, he or she can block out most or all of your message. It is important that the message is structured and delivered so that this does not happen. The basic structure conforms to the pattern established before, but it has been fine tuned to help you deliver the message in a way that should improve its chance of being received and understood as you intend.

Giving Feedback To Others

- Explain the general area you want to talk about.
- Explain why what you are about to say is important.
- Try to find an example of positive behavior to set a positive tone.
- Be specific, and use examples.
- Describe what happened first, but don't judge. For example, "You didn't make the deadline; and, as a result, the client was upset."
- Concentrate on specific things that can be improved or changed.
- Agree on future action to prevent a repeat of the problems.
- Determine that your message has been clearly understood by asking open questions.

Involve the other person

Facts and events, rather than the person's characteristics, should be stressed. When you start to address the specific problem, if possible, try to get the individual concerned to identify the problem, rather than your doing so. He or she may realize that things have not gone well and know why. In most cases, people do have a reasonable idea about what went wrong. To help them to identify the problems you can use open questions and active listening. For example, "How do you think the project you did went last week? What were the areas you found caused you problems?"

This approach allows them to talk through what happened. Further questions can point them in the right direction. For example, " You seemed to take a lot of time on the report. What were the problems you had?" You can also offer assistance, such as, "Well, you seemed to have problems writing a report. What were they and how can I help you to overcome them?"

In other cases the person concerned is genuinely unaware that there has been a problem. This situation requires even more delicate handling. If at all possible, try to introduce a negative with a positive. "I would like to talk about how I can help you to improve your report writing because there are a few mistakes in the one you recently submitted."

The annual appraisal

Because the communication of information about their own performance is so important to people, and has such a great impact on their motivation and development, you should consider how best to handle such feedback. The way that a message is delivered is critical to its understanding and acceptance. This applies just as much to the appraisal as to any other communication situation.

Your organization may already have an appraisal process, but you should not just "go through the motions."

An appraisal is an opportunity to help the person to improve. Preparation is crucial. Make notes about the points you want to get across. If the appraisal is expected to take an hour, spend at least 20 minutes reading the relevant notes, deciding what you want to say, and thinking through the points to be discussed. Consider possible solutions to any problems.

When the person who is being appraised arrives, help him or her relax. Many people find the annual appraisal unnerving. You will not achieve much if the other person is a nervous wreck. Explain what is going to happen, how performance is being assessed, and how any measures of performance are worked out. Stress that you are appraising to provide help and support, not to find fault.

Then move onto more general issues, but keep the focus on facts rather than on opinions. Follow the basic guidelines for giving feedback. In each area that needs improvement, agree to a plan of action. Also set deadlines by which targets will be met. It is essential that this is agreed upon by both parties.

At the end, always give the other person the chance to raise any issues and to ask you questions. Get some feedback about what he or she thought of the appraisal and how you conducted it. Did it help with identifying strengths and weaknesses? Did you do most of the talking? Did you use open questions?

It may be worth considering the introduction of "interim" appraisals, perhaps midway between the annual appraisals. People will find it helpful, and it shows that you are committed to their development and improvement.

Don't put it off

Although it may be tempting, do not put off giving negative feedback. It is all too easy to try to avoid the potential awkwardness and conflict that may arise from presenting negative feedback. After all, we all want to be liked, but people also need to know when they are not performing well. On many occasions the individual or team doesn't realize that things are going wrong. You are helping them to improve, which, in the end, will be appreciated.

Communicating By Telephone

Remember that people get tired of wasting their time on unproductive telephone calls. If you can make every call productive you will become one of the most effective people in your organization.

Even if you do not use the telephone to directly generate business, it is essential to be able to use it effectively. It is vital that calls from outside the organization are handled well. To the caller, *you* are the organization. How you handle the call creates an image of the whole company.

Calls from within your organization matter as much as those from people outside. This presents an image of your department, your team, and you.

On the telephone the nonverbal signals used to help get a message across in face to face communication, such as facial expressions, are clearly not present. All of the signals are in the voice and the vocabulary.

Answer the call within four rings and with a smile! This confirms that you are efficient, and the smile will ensure that you sound positive when you answer. You may not feel like smiling; but the facial muscles you use in a smile affect the tone of your voice, making it sound more positive.

The verbal handshake Introduce yourself and, if you are the one making the call, establish whether it is a convenient time to talk. This is particularly important if you are calling a mobile phone. The person taking the call may be in an inconvenient place. If the call is to a hands-free car phone, for example, other people may be listening.

HAS THE CALL BEEN SUCCESSFUL?

Think about what annoys you when you try to contact people by telephone. Here are some general things that tend to have an influence on the caller's impression.

- Whether the call is answered at all
- How long it takes to answer the call
- How many people the caller speaks to before it is possible to speak to the right one
- Whether the person taking the call listens to what the caller has to say
- How polite the response is
- Whether the call is answered with courtesy and efficiency
- Whether the call is productive
- If both parties agree on the outcome and action
- Pressing lots of buttons and listening to automated voices, yet never speaking to a human being
- Talking to someone for a long time before finding out that they are not the right person to help
- Not being given the opportunity to explain what it is you really want

Taking ownership If you take responsibility for the call, the person calling will be more relaxed. This means that you agree to take action on their behalf, that you will see that the person who is responsible does so, or that you will transfer the call to the proper person. Accept that you represent your organization, department, or team, and follow up to see if the agreed outcome actually happens. How many times have you been infuriated to hear, "I'm sorry that's not my area," or "I'm afraid I haven't the authority to deal with this."

Keep the call on track Make the caller feel involved. Use the caller's name, ask open questions (those that begin with what, where, how, which, when, and who) to encourage them to talk. Make appropriate sounds to confirm that you are still paying attention, such as, "Yes" and "I understand." These replace the visual signals you use when communicating face to face. This is particularly important if the person calling is making a complaint or explaining a problem.

Record and repeat Write down what the caller is saying, and verify that you have it correctly. This confirms to the caller that you have understood what has been said. If the conversation is likely to be

PUTTING CALLS ON HOLD

Before you put a caller on hold or transfer a call, let the caller know what is going to happen. Give the name and number of the person to whom you are transferring the caller in case the call gets cut off. Make sure that the caller understands why the transfer is necessary. For example, say, "I am going to transfer you to Jim Benton, the product manager, on extension 334 because he deals with the type of information you need. There may be a moment or two of silence as the call goes through."

either long or complex, write down the main points in bullet form during the call. This will allow you to repeat and give you a record of the main points for reference after the call is finished. Use the principles of active listening to find out what the caller really wants.

Closing the call This stage is essentially an opportunity to provide the caller with any extra information they may need, to agree to any action that will be taken, and to clarify the deadline. Give the caller your name and extension number, so that he or she can get back to you if necessary, and take their phone number. If you agree to do something during the call, write it down as soon as the call has finished. How many times have you forgotten something you agreed to do in a telephone call? If you need to, send the caller written confirmation of what has been promised.

Using The Written Word

The same basic principles that apply to verbal communication also apply to written communication. You must decide the message you want to get across, find the best means to deliver it, and make the delivery. It is as important with written messages as with verbal ones to confirm that they have been received and understood.

A written message gives you a permanent record. This "hard copy" can be useful. It can be referred to at any time and sent to any number of people. Written communication allows you to communicate complex ideas and information in a format that lets the recipient assimilate it at his or her own pace and style.

If your message is personal or complex, maybe doing it in person would be preferable even if you then send written confirmation later.

If you feel awkward talking to people, try to do it more often using the formats in this book to help you do it well and build your confidence. By avoiding speaking to people directly and relying instead on written communication you will isolate yourself and may lose touch with your team because two-way communication will be avoided. If you do not receive feedback, this may cause problems in the future.

The main forms of written communication you will probably be using at work are letters, memos (including e-mail), and reports. Most of us have to reply regularly to letters or to initiate them. Even if you don't, you certainly will have to send and reply to letters in your personal life. This section should help you in both areas.

STAY IN TOUCH
Do not use e-mail or memos as a way of avoiding face to face communication. Avoiding talking to people can lead to problems in the future.

Letters

Any letter you send (this includes e-mail) must follow the general rules of effective communication. Be simple, clear, and concise; and follow the logical structure of all communications.

Before you begin, clarify the objective of your letter. Ask yourself, "What do I want to achieve with this letter?" Try to get the message across in a way that ensures that the person receiving it will understand it. Keep the language simple. Use plain English with no jargon. Keep the letter as simple and to the point as possible. Try not to leave the reader in doubt as to what you want the outcome to be.

It may help to imagine what you would say if you spoke to the person instead of putting your thoughts on paper. This seems obvious, but many people have difficulty putting on paper what they would have no trouble saying face to face.

Plan the letter before you begin to write it. Write the headings suggested by Kipling's poem *Six Honest Serving Men* (page 36) on a rough piece of paper, and write out a draft.

What do I want to achieve? This is the purpose of the letter. What do you want to say to the person who will be getting the letter? If you want them to do something, what exactly is it?

Why do I want this to happen? What is the reason for writing the letter? What caused you to want to achieve the objective? It's often a good idea to give brief background information on the problem or question.

When? Are there any time limits? Next week, next month, or next year? When do you want it completed by?

How? Do you want to achieve your objective in a particular way, or will you leave it up to the other person?

Where? Are there geographical or physical factors? Where do you want the meeting to be held? Where should the letter be delivered?

To whom am I going to say it? In most cases you know who the letter is going to; but, occasionally, you may not know the person's name. If possible, try to find out the correct name. "Dear sir" will work, but using a name will immediately encourage a positive response. If you have made the effort to use the name of the person to whom you are writing, this will make the contents more personal. Also consider if you need to copy the letter to other people.

Using The Written Word

FINE TUNE THE MESSAGE
Having clarified your message, fine tune it before you put it in letter form to ensure that the reader understands exactly what you want. The acronym, SCRAP, will help:
- Situation
- Consequences
- Resolution
- Action
- Politeness

Situation Sum up what the letter is about by stating the facts. For example, "Last week your delivery was late."

Consequences include a development from the facts and a resulting problem or question. For example, "This is not the first time this has happened; and, as a result, we could not complete the job."

Resolution Suggest a possible solution. "We understand that your delivery van was caught in traffic and that the required time is now lengthened. Perhaps, if the drivers left earlier this would remedy the problem."

Action is what you will do or expect the person getting the letter to do. For example, "Would you please ensure that your delivery van leaves early enough to get our delivery to us on time."

Politeness Even if you are upset with the person or organization to whom the letter is being sent, remain polite, and concentrate on the facts. If you use emotional language or insults, you are unlikely to get a positive response. Try, "Would you please try to ensure that our deliveries arrive on time in future." Conclude with some expression of goodwill, or at least be polite, even if it is only a basic "sincerely yours."

MEMOS
Memos are part of business life and can play a useful part in getting information across in a brief form. A memo can be used as a quick written confirmation of what happened in a conversation or meeting. A memo should be like a short, crisp letter, not a rambling, jargon-filled treatise. Use the SCRAP format, but keep it very short.

Ensuring that the job gets done

On occasion, perhaps after a team meeting, you need to confirm who is to do what by when, and who will receive the report. This can become complicated. To make clear what is to happen, you can set up an action schedule at the end of the meeting. Record the information in a simple table. The action schedule can be referred to for more detail in the minutes. It will make it absolutely clear who is responsible for certain activities.

All of those who have to complete some action should be given or sent a copy of the schedule. It is often included in the minutes of more formal meetings and is sent to everyone who attended. To enable those with assignments to complete them on time, the minutes or schedules should be published in ample time for the job to be completed.

In the final analysis, the purpose of communication is to achieve something. It should be made clear what has been decided and, if anything has to be done, who it must be done by. This is what the action schedule is about. Without it, meetings are just "gab fests" that waste the time of all of the involved.

EXAMPLE ACTION SCHEDULE

Actions schedule for Stage 1 of marketing plan

Action:	Responsible:	By:	Confirm to:
Contact top 15 clients	DJP	October 14	Head of Mkt.
Submit advertising text	PGH	October 22	Head of Mkt.
Produce graphics	DB	October 22	PGH
Approve advertising	Head of Mkt/MD	October 31	–

Writing A Report

Writing a report can be a daunting prospect, realize that you are being trusted with something that is important to the organization. If you think there is a problem that needs addressing, you could offer to write a report about it.

Many people are promoted after writing a good report that solved a problem. Even if this does not happen, writing a report will at least mean that you understand the organization.

Reports follow some of the logical structure of letters; but, because they are usually longer than letters, some additional rules apply. If your organization has a standard format, follow it; but also include all of the ingredients given below.

1. Give the present position. Summarize the current situation. Cover the general background in order to put the report in context.

2. Outline the problems involved. This is probably why the report is being written.

3. Detail the possibilities. Enumerate the possible courses of action, and evaluate them. It is important that there are a range of possibilities, including do nothing, preserve the status quo, or change to something else.

4. Make your proposals. This is the place to sell your ideas. You have to make the proposal attractive to the reader. Do not be tempted to omit this section because it might upset someone or be incorrect. As long as your report is logical and you use a methodical approach, this should not be a problem. If what you propose will have a financial cost, outline the projected costs and stress the benefits.

The tips on page 72, *Negotiating and Getting Agreement,* for persuading sceptics to give your ideas a try are useful in reports as well.

The proposal is the main body of the report. Keep the language simple and concise, making sure it is relevant to the problem and the points raised in the report so far. Avoid jargon, and use plain English. Choose short words if possible.

Keep sentences and paragraphs short. Bear in mind that you want your report to be read. Pages and pages of solid text are intimidating and boring. Try to help the reader in the way you lay out the pages. Use indents, wide margins, and logical headings and subheadings. Try to use graphics, such as charts and tables, to help to put across complex information.

This structure covers the main body of the report. The other parts of the report may not be familiar to you, but they all play an important part.

Summary

Include a one- or two-paragraph summary of the whole report. It allows someone who does not have time to read the whole report to understand the present position, problem, possibilities, and your proposal. It can be difficult to get all this into such a small space, but it is an essential part of any report. Write this section last.

Terms of Reference

This outlines the instructions you were given to write the report and directly links to the objective. Include information about who asked you to write the report and what limits you were given – what you consider were the "rules of engagement" for your report.

Objective

This is the reason for the report. For example, "to identify a cost-effective solution to the current ventilation equipment problem."

Bibliography and sources

Refer to any books or articles you have used by listing them and referencing them in the bibliography. Sources (discussions with other people, rather than published information) should also be given. Include dates because information can become dated.

Appendices

Extra information that supports the main body of the report – such as data, case studies, results of other reports that contribute to your proposal but are too long to go into the main text – should be provided as appendices. These tend to be the basic research findings. The contents of the appendices should be referred to at the appropriate point in the main body of the report.

Making a final check

After spell-checking, read the report a couple of times with a break in between; and get someone else to read it, as well.

To help you determine what goes into the appendices ask yourself, "Does the reader HAVE to have this information to make the decision?" If the answer is "yes," it should be in the main body. If the answer is "no," put it in the appendices.

THE FORMAT
Having written the main body of your report, package it correctly by adding the other components. The final structure should follow this pattern.

> **Title page**
> **Contents page**
> **Summary** (sometimes called Executive Summary)
> **Terms of Reference**
> **Acknowledgements**
> **Objective**
> **Main body of report:**
> > **Present position**
> > **Problem**
> > **Possibilities**
> > **Proposal**
> **Bibliography and sources**
> **Appendices**

Negotiating And Getting Agreement

Trying to persuade a skeptical person – whoever they may be – to accept your proposals is an important area of communication. This may be about asking him to change what he does, requesting more resources, changing existing systems, or taking a different view. Whether you are working with team members, peers, your boss, or clients, you need to get across the critical information that will allow them to agree to what you want.

One of the most awkward communication areas is that of discussing problems and trying to reach agreement. We have already looked at giving negative feedback, which is a related area. In this section we look at how to communicate effectively in those general problem situations. These might include any area where there may be conflicting views or contradictory objectives, such as negotiating resources from your boss or getting extra work from your team.

Encourage people to consider problems they may have.

The first step is to get everyone involved to agree that there is a problem and it is worth discussing. It is important to get people to try to identify their own problems, rather than simply telling them what is wrong. This approach stops them from feeling that you have identified problems they don't think really exist and, as a consequence, ignoring your message.

By asking open questions (how, why, what) you should be able to get other people to focus on what the problem is and enable them to find solutions. It is much better for the people concerned and for your working relationship if you can help them to solve their own problems, instead of telling them what to do.

If someone has difficulty identifying problems or finding answers, try asking more questions to help them to pinpoint the problem area. For example, you could ask, "How do you think I could help you develop your skills in the technical areas?" Once they start to talk about their perceptions of the situation, use active listening skills to help them come to a fuller understanding of the problem and find solutions.

Play fair. People view "forcing them" or "conning them" to give you what you want, as a quick fix in these situations. Neither is effective in the long term. Forcing someone to do something he does not want to will just cause a working relationship to sour, and "conning" people will only work for a short time. Then, you will not be trusted again. Put yourself in the position of the other people involved. Would you agree to your own proposals as you have presented them? What benefit will the other people involved gain from agreement? In practical terms, you have to "sell" your proposal.

TACTICS THAT MAY HELP TO PERSUADE OTHERS TO TRY OUT YOUR IDEAS OR SUGGESTIONS

■ Request a short "test" period. This does not commit others to a long-term commitment and will allow them further time to consider. It also gives you a chance to prove that your ideas work.

■ Confirm the overall benefits of your proposal both to the organization and to the team or individual you are trying to convince. If you can establish that there is a benefit, the chance of getting what you want are much greater. If you can, prove the benefits your proposal would produce. Make use of the following where appropriate:

Use your own figures and data to support your argument.

Give examples of places where a similar approach has been successful.

Provide evidence of support from other people or senior staff.

Show why your proposal is an improvement over the status quo.

Show that it would be possible to evaluate the outcome of your idea.

Show why the subject of the proposal is important.

Show that any costs incurred are outweighed by the benefits.

Make the proposal simple to understand and clear in its reasoning.

5

Identify needs
Action plan
Take action
Develop skills

Where do I need to improve?

How can I develop my skills?

Do I need support?

Developing Your Skills

To get maximum benefit from this section of the book it is important to complete all the exercises in it. They will enable you to build on the self-assessment you have already done and plan how to improve your skills.

You will identify areas in which you should improve your skills, prioritize them, and make a personal development plan to help you improve. You will also consider how you could help improve the communication skills of your team members.

Watch yourself in action

The self-assessment questionnaires in chapter two will have given you an indication of how good your current skills are. To improve, assess your own performance from day to day and week to week.

Each time you communicate observe what you do, record how it went, and evaluate what was good and what could have been better. This doesn't have to be a large report – just a few notes on a piece of paper about what happened and ideas for improvement. It should take about five minutes and is well worth the time. Slips of paper tend to get lost; so, if you have a desk planner, jot down ideas for self-improvement or team enhancement.

Where do I need to improve ?

Draw up a self-assessment table following the example given (right). Transfer the ratings you got in the self-assessments in chapter two. Be honest when you complete the list.

The exercise will be more accurate if you also get feedback from others – your team, peers, boss, and friends. Ask them if you communicate clearly. Do you ever miss out on information or confuse them? Do you ask them if they have understood your message? Do you give your team feedback effectively whether it is praise or negative feedback? You could also try tape recording meetings, conversations, telephone calls, and other verbal communication. Explain why you are doing it, and ask the other people involved for their permission. Your team will probably agree because it should improve your communication skills, which should help them too.

How did you do?

You will probably have identified at least three or four areas in which you need to improve your skills; any fewer than this means either you are a brilliant communicator or you were not being as honest as you could be. The next step is to produce a specific plan to develop each skill where improvement is necessary. If time permits, try to improve the skills you classified as "satisfactory." Why be satisfactory when you can be good?

Repeat this assessment regularly – possible every six months to a year.

Skills	Good	Satisfactory	Could Be Better
Understanding the principles of communication			
Planning a message			
Matching my message to the recipient			
Face-to-face communication with individuals			
Face-to-face communication with groups			
Giving positive feedback			
Giving negative feedback			
Using the telephone			
Briefing a team			
Running team meetings			
Letter writing			
Memo writing			
Writing reports			
Communicating with your boss			
Communicating with your peers			
Active listening and questioning others to be sure you understand them			
Talking through problems and getting agreement			

Areas Of Regular Communication

What about the communications you undertake regularly? Are you communicating effectively by using the right message and method for the situation? Do you get your message across effectively to all of those with whom you have to communicate? If not, you may be wasting time and resources. Having considered the general strengths and weaknesses in the way you communicate, think about the main communication events in which you engage at work.

It is important to focus your development plans on areas of weakness that relate to the most important activities you do at work. For example, it is unfortunate if you do not accurately express yourself when you order stationery; but, if you cannot explain to your production team how you would like productivity to be improved, this is much more serious.

By constructing a communication event list you will be able to consider all of the major communication areas in your working life and to analyze your performance in each. Use the example communication event list (right) to consider how you could improve. Set up the table as shown, and put in each main communication activity you engage in, along with the way you do it. For each event ask yourself the following questions: Are you using the best means of communication? Does the message get across? Do you receive feedback?

To check that you have assessed it correctly, why not ask the people with whom you communicate for their opinion of your performance?

This exercise can be particularly useful if you have to use a wide range of different communication methods. Can you identify areas where you could improve communication by adding or changing the means of delivery or the content of your messages? For example, in area three in the communication event list (right), perhaps adding an extra communication channel would improve relationships with clients and thus increase sales. In area four it may be a good idea to practice making the message clearer by getting feedback from the team. In example five, the level of understanding with the boss could possibly be improved with the use of open and closed questions and active listening.

EXAMPLE COMMUNICATION EVENT LIST					
Event	With whom are you communicating?	Communication method	Is this the best medium?	Is there any feedback?	Is the message usually successful?
1 Weekly sales figures	Peter Smith	Verbal, 1-on-1	Yes	No	Tends to be rushed
2 Liaison with minor clients	Minor clients	Telephone	Yes	No	Partially
3 Sending out information to clients	Major clients	Written	Possibly	Only with verbal follow up	Partially, but needs telephone follow up
4 Giving feedback to team on performance	All team members	Verbal	Yes	Yes, but they say I am not always clear on what I want from them	Partially
5 Weekly meeting with boss	Boss	Verbal, 1-on-1	Yes	Yes	Partially, but we need to be clearer
6 Contact with other departments	Various	Verbal Telephone Written	Possibly, but perhaps I don't write down as much as I should	Yes, but occasional confusion about timing and responsibilities	Partially, but we need to agree things so that both sides are clear on actions

Preparing To Write A Development Plan

Once you have identified the areas in which you wish to develop your skills, put together a plan for improvement. First, use the model below to consider how you learn. Then, review your experiences, and learn from your assessment. The next step is to plan your development. This should not be a one-time event that you do only while reading this book. To really develop you should use this circle as often as possible.

Briefly review your experiences as they occur. Then, every six-to-twelve months, sit down, assess yourself, and write out a formal development plan for the next period. Use the exercises in the book to help in your self-assessment and development planning regularly throughout your career.

Self-assessment will help you discover where your weaknesses lie. A model called the *Johari Window* (opposite page) can help you think about this more clearly. It suggests that there are four areas of information about ourselves, and we need to consider all of them to understand how to improve.

Information known to yourself and others
This is public knowledge. Perhaps everyone in the office knows that you are the best person to deal with a certain difficult client. Think about why you are the best at particular communication issues. What is it about your approach in those situations that works? What do you do that is different from what other people do?

THE LEARNING CIRCLE

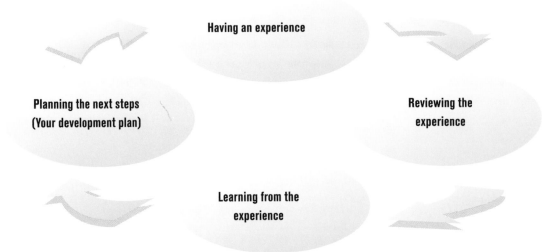

Having an experience

Reviewing the experience

Learning from the experience

Planning the next steps
(Your development plan)

Information not known to others What things do you alone know about yourself? For example, do you feel shy in groups but manage to cover this up when you are at work by avoiding meetings? Are there ways you could help yourself overcome this problem?

Information known only to others. Try to find out the things others know about you, but you don't know. This is your blind spot. For example, have you ever learned from someone else that you have a habit you were unaware of? Perhaps you scratch your ear or nose while you talk. Watching yourself on video can highlight such habits, such as saying "er" at the start of each sentence.

Discovering your blind spot emphasizes the importance of getting feedback, not just from your boss, but also from your staff and peers. There may be a range of things you do that affect the team, the individuals in it, and their performance.

Information not known This is the information no one knows as yet. It can only be revealed through some kind of self-analysis or discovery, which may sound a little psychological and intimidating. It need not be. For example, in your life have you ever discovered that you are good at something you would never even have imagined? Perhaps you took up a hobby through your children and discovered a real talent; or you have found that you enjoy working on computers, though you were trained late in your career. Such discoveries fall into this category.

You probably already have ideas about how you work with people, what you do well, and where you may be weak. Is there a pattern behind this? What jobs don't you enjoy? Why do you dislike them? What can you do to change your attitude? If you feel intimidated by some people, who are they and why do you feel that way? How can you solve that problem? Thinking carefully about these issues will probably reveal information about you that was previously part of the "unknown at present" area. By analyzing your problems and uncovering the causes, you will find the answer and be better able to tackle them.

	JOHARI WINDOW	
Known to You	**Public Knowledge**	**Secret Knowledge**
Not Known to You	**Your Blind Spot**	**Unknown at Present**
	Known to Other People	**Not Known to Other People**

Identifying Development Needs

By now, you have identified how good you are in each of the communication areas and in the regular communication activities you undertake. Now you can use all that information to improve your effectiveness in your problem areas.

For example, if you have identified a problem with putting together your message in all areas of communication, you might write "need to use format from book to make sure my message is clear." If you keep forgetting to ask for feedback after one-to-one communications, write, "forget to ask for feedback; need to remember to practice listening, and to make careful use of open questions."

The chart gives an idea of the steps to take to improve your skills. Expand it to produce your own detailed development action plan.

Area of communication	Things you need to do to improve
Understanding the principles of communication	
Putting together your message	
Face-to-face communication with individuals	
Face-to-face communication with groups	
Giving feedback	
Using the telephone	
Briefing a team	
Running team meetings	
Using voicemail/answering machines	
Letter/memo writing	
Writing reports	
Communicating with your boss	
Active listening and questioning of others to be sure you understand them	
Talking through problems and getting agreement	
Other Areas	

Development Action Plan

Select the areas in which you need improvement and the steps you would take. Then, make a copy of the Development Action Plan for each specific area.

1. Note the skill you need to improve. This may be "Need to take more care in communicating with inexperienced staff; tend to give them insufficient detail, which means they can become confused."

2. Outline the steps needed to improve. For example, "Write out the appropriate format from the book, and prepare in advance for one-to-one discussions about important matters".

3. Decide whether your boss or organization could help you to improve. If any of the actions you propose would be more effective with support from your boss or the company, include what they could do to help. For example, "Discuss with my boss how she may have dealt with a problem similar to the ones I regularly encounter."

4. Enter the date by which you will have achieved an improvement or will have completed the action you have assigned yourself. You must establish a deadline, and stick to it. If you don't, you may suddenly find years have passed; you have done nothing to improve; and, as a result, someone else has been selected for promotion. Remember that it is up to you to develop yourself. No one else will do it, although a good boss may help.

Development Action Plan

Development need:

Actions by:

You	Your boss

Organizational support?

To be completed/achieved by:

Immediate Action Plan

You may find that your Development Action Plan identifies improvements that will take some months to show results. To keep yourself motivated, try to achieve something as quickly as possible. For example, "Write down main points of message before important face to face meetings," or "Seek feedback on my performance," can be implemented right away. It may help to draw up an Immediate Action Plan made up of steps from your Development Action Plan that can be taken at once.

Try to find at least six improvement actions to take immediately, possibly including the four already given in the example. Both you and your team will show an immediate benefit, and your team will be motivated and encouraged by your improvement.

Promoting development and flexibility

The workplace is not static, and individuals and teams constantly need to develop their skills to meet the challenges of the future. These challenges may be the result of technological developments, changes in legislation, the introduction of new systems, or other factors that demand updating and improving skills. If people do not pass on their skills and knowledge effectively then they will take their expertise and know-how with them when they leave, your company will lose valuable resources.

If you can encourage the more experienced team members to communicate effectively, especially in giving feedback, they will help the development of others and even supervise that development. Asking

	Steps to Take	Notes
1	Identify areas where my communication skills can be improved, and produce a written development plan to achieve this step.	
2	Set up meeting to discuss personal development plan to improve my communication skills with my manager. Explain the support I would like to help me achieve my objectives.	
3	Start improving my communication at once by using the formats in the book.	
4	Introduce team briefings every week or two weeks.	

someone to help with the development of another individual is one of the highest compliments you, as a boss, can bestow. It demonstrates your confidence in him or her and can serve to improve performance greatly.

Giving individual support

Draw up a team-development plan by assessing how team members perform in each of the main communication areas in which they need to improve their skills. Obviously, some will not be appropriate. A new recruit may not be required to write a report but may need to answer the phone, confirm orders with suppliers, and write memos. More experienced workers may have to give feedback to others, deal with other departments, write reports, or run meetings. Your "next in command" should have the same communication skills as you have.

When you see where team members need help, discuss this with them and come to an agreement. Use the book's plan formats to plan the development of each individual. Helping team members to develop will also improve motivation within the team.

Review and update the development plans at regular intervals.

DEVELOPING COMMUNICATION IN YOUR TEAM

If all of the members of the team are helped to improve their communication, they will understand the principles and be better prepared to communicate with you in an open way. This means you will have a more accurate view of what is going on, find out about problems sooner, and be able to delegate tasks that involve communication in a way you may not have done previously. Try to improve the communication skills of all your team members. Better communication between team members will bring benefits in the following areas:

- Better understanding of your communication
- More feedback
- Better and faster skills development
- More effective problem solving
- Better motivation and self-confidence
- Reduced misunderstandings; saving time and resources
- Greater mutual support and cooperation
- Higher knowledge levels within team
- More flexible response

Don't delay do it today

Help Your Boss To Communicate With You

Your relationship with your boss is as important as that with your team, so spend time getting it right. Effective communication builds trust and if you trust each other in your working relationship, it will benefit both of you. Helping your boss to communicate effectively with you will make life easier for both of you. If you feel that your boss does not understand you, does not communicate effectively, does not delegate effectively and so on, stop blaming the boss and try to think about it more logically. Perhaps your boss also has a boss who does not communicate effectively. What problems

HERE ARE A FEW SUGGESTIONS ON COMMUNICATING WITH YOUR BOSS MORE EFFECTIVELY. PERHAPS YOU COULD DISCUSS HOW YOU CAN DO THE FOLLOWING:

■ Make life easy for your boss to do their job. Keep them informed about what is going on – not everything but make sure that they have the information they need and stick to deadlines.

■ Take a positive attitude to your boss – respond positively even if you are not convinced and talk it through.

■ Prepare ground for discussions in advance so you both know what is on the agenda.

■ Consider that your boss has problems too – see the whole picture, not just your own concerns.

■ Don't give your boss nasty surprises, talk through problems in good time to avoid a last minute rush.

■ If there is a difficult job to do even if you don't really want your team to do it, once agreement has been reached with your boss defend the decision as your own. Do not say "The boss wants you to…"

■ Discuss your development plans – the boss needs to support you in these – so he or she needs to know about them.

does your boss have? Do you see the whole picture? Do you ever ask your boss about what is going on elsewhere, or use open questions and active listening to help communication between you?

You need to help your boss to help you. If he or she is worrying about what you or your team is doing, you are probably being pestered with enquiries about whether or not things are going well. If you make sure that he or she knows what is going on, you will probably be given more freedom.

Discuss how you can communicate effectively with each other. As a first step you can tell him or her about your development plan and ask for help. Do your own assessment of your boss's communication ability using the format you used to identify your strengths and weaknesses before you meet so that you know which areas to concentrate on, but be diplomatic.

MISTAKES
Everyone worries about making mistakes and being exposed to negative feedback from superiors as a result. If your communication is poor, you and your team will probably make more mistakes. If a mistake happens, ask yourself, "Was it my own communication that allowed this mistake to happen?"

Once your boss is thinking about communication discuss all of the areas with them, identify problems and find solutions for mutual benefit. What are the areas of communication where the confusion creeps in? Try to negotiate a solution which benefits both of you.

You and your boss are a team, aiming for the same goals. To achieve what you want to you need to work effectively together. If you can communicate well, you will work well together.

6

Improve culture
Team briefings
Help your boss
Further ideas

Can my skills develop further?

How can I improve team communication?

Can I help improve my team's skills?

Improve Communications With Team Briefings

It is not an understatement to say that the communication within an organization – the degree to which people really are able to get their messages across – sets the tone for the whole organization. If you don't feel you can get your feelings across, or you feel no one listens to you, you become demotivated and will not work as hard as you could. Faulty communication also leads to more mistakes, as well as time and resources being lost or wasted.

Effective communication is the key to the culture within the organization. If it is present, the culture will be good, and people will work well together. If it is not, the organization will not work well, and, inevitably, profits will suffer.

The same applies to your team. If teammates communicate effectively with each other and with you, they will work better together. In the final analysis, even if the rest of the organization has poor communication, there is no reason why your team should. Do not worry about the rest of them. At least your team will function effectively, and your success may start to change the way others work.

A good way to improve communication and culture is through regular, useful, team briefings.

Team Briefings

We have seen that you can improve team performance by helping all of the team members communicate with you – expressing their ideas, feelings, and views. In addition to doing this on a day-to-day basis, you may find it useful to have regular team meetings. (see page 56 *Face-to-Face With A Group*). You can take this further – and gain more benefit – by using regular, structured team briefings. This does not mean only that you brief the team, but that the team also gives its input on important issues or asks questions. The advice given for communicating face to face with a group can be used in any situation and should ensure that the message gets across. With a regular, more structured team briefing you can cover a whole range of issues, as opposed to one specific issue, that must be resolved. By holding regular team briefings, you will keep everyone informed about how they are doing and what is going on in the organization. It also gives the team members a chance to provide you with feedback and to resolve any areas of misunderstanding by asking questions. Use the following format to help you get maximum benefit from your team briefings.

Progress & Performance One of the most important questions for both teams and individuals is, "How are we doing?" It may be difficult for you to provide a specific figure, but an indication of how things are going is helpful. If you use technical words or statistics, be sure that they are understood by all. If anyone does not understand, you have failed to communicate. The team briefing may be a good forum to praise people for outstanding performance – if it is directly related to an item under discussion.

Policy & plans In this section you can explain existing policies and future plans. Since we are sometimes unsure about why things happened or are done in a certain way, briefings allow you to explain such things to the team. In addition, we all like to know what is going to happen in the future; so, if possible, explain any possible future plans, even if they are not yet fully decided or implemented.

It is much better to give the team the correct information than to let them make up their own or to have them rely on rumors.

People The briefing session can confirm promotions, moves, changes in responsibilities, and roles. It can also allow you to publicly praise the work of the team or an individual if you have not done so already under "progress and performance." For example, you can mention the fact that someone has passed a professional exam. This kind of recognition can substantially improve staff motivation and morale.

Points for action This section will cover anything that should be done in the future. Remember to make clear what has to be done, by whom, and when. It is often advisable, if it has been a fairly complicated meeting that covered a range of topics, to send out a detailed action schedule to everyone who attended the meeting. Having it in writing ensures that everyone is aware of what was agreed upon and what their responsibilities are. The schedule should include deadlines by which tasks should be complete.

Improve Communications With Team Briefings

Feedback This is one of the most important parts of the briefing because it allows the team to present ideas or to ask questions. You may find it useful to anticipate possible questions so that you can have answers prepared. For example, you may have discovered in the previous week that there is a specific matter worrying some members of the team. Find out as much as you can before the briefing, as it is probable that the subject will come up. This also allows you to deal with it at one time, thus saving multiple explanations and letting everyone know what is going on, simultaneously.

There may be questions to which you do not know the answers. These should be passed on to the person who can answer them. If there is not a full team-briefing system in place, you will probably have to persuade the relevant person to answer the questions so that you will be able to keep your team informed of the latest developments.

STRUCTURE YOUR TEAM BRIEFING IN THE FOLLOWING WAY

1 Progress and performance

2 Policy and plans

3 People

4 Points for action

5 Feedback

Open Communication And Learning

To be effective in any job, we have to be able to improve our skills and to develop professionally. Communication hastens this process by enabling the knowledge of the more experienced or proficient employees to be made available to those who can benefit from it. Everyone learns by trial and error or by using knowledge they have gained from others. Trial and error can be costly in terms of time spent to achieve a successful outcome because mistakes are made and resources wasted. By passing on knowledge, these problems can be avoided.

Many organizations have found that if everyone can be encouraged to communicate their learning and ideas freely, things get done faster, and there are fewer problems. In addition, people develop skills faster which allows more delegation and less "fire fighting."

If you can achieve effective communication within the team, you can develop it into a "learning team." This means that everyone takes responsibility for the development of themselves and the other people. The free communication of information, advice, and support within the team permits learning to take place much more quickly than normal.

Apply some simple principles to building a learning team:

■ Understand each other's strengths and weaknesses, and use them to help.
■ Assess the areas in which the exchange of information is most needed.
■ Have a team development plan and individual development plans.
■ Think of the things you have in common (objectives, team spirit) and the things that are different (specialist skills) as strengths you use.
■ Design a map of how information can be transferred between team members.
■ Always link team learning to business and personal goals.
■ Reward and recognize team members who help others on the team learn.

Further self development

You may wish to develop your communication skills further. You can achieve this through ongoing self-assessment, feedback from others, training courses, and reading other books. Above all, you must put your ideas and discoveries into practice.

This book is also an ongoing aid to your development. Do not just leave it on the shelf, once you have read it. Go back to it on a regular basis to assess how you have improved and where further progress can be made.

Development is not a one-time event. The people who do well are those who continuously improve their skills.

General Development Suggestions

These are a few general suggestions that will help you develop your abilities, not only in communication, but in a wide range of other useful skills.

Role models and mentors

Many people have found that a role model or mentor can help them to develop their skills very effectively. First, what is the difference between the two? A role model is someone whose behavior you copy because they do what you think are the right things. Your role model may be a successful person whose position you aspire to. Adopting a role model can be an effective tool for self-improvement, but there is always a danger of copying poor behavior. Do not forget you are not a clone; adapt what your role model does to your own style. If you don't, it may become obvious that you are copying someone else, which, in turn, may give the impression that you are "putting on an act."

In contrast, a mentor works with you to give you support when you need it and to help you find solutions to your problems. This is particularly important when you are trying to develop your interpersonal skills. This means that you can actually access and use the mental assets of a more skilled and experienced person, benefitting from the time they invested in achieving that level of knowledge.

Finding a mentor can be one of the most effective of all forms of development, especially when it is combined with self-analysis and development planning.

If you are given the chance to work with a mentor, who you respect and who can give you the benefit of his or her experience and skills to help you develop, grab the opportunity with both hands. If your organization sets up a mentoring system and asks for volunteers, go for it!

OTHER SUGGESTIONS

Think about your relationships with those you work with (the team, boss, and peers). Are they open and positive working relationships?

The importance of taking a positive approach to problems and people cannot be underestimated.

Anticipate problems from team members, peers, or bosses; ensure that you tackle problems early – before they have gone too far.

Do not be afraid to seek help and guidance from trusted colleagues or a mentor.

Do not rush into anything. Always take a logical approach using the ideas and suggestions in this book. A cautious approach increases the chances of doing something well and reduces the chances of a disaster!

Conclusion

Communicating well is all about people. It is getting your message across effectively to others and having others get their message across to you. If you make the effort to communicate with others as individuals, matching your style to theirs, they will feel that you are respecting them and they will return that respect.

If you use the ideas in this book and invest a little effort in improving your skills, you will be surprised at how quickly and well your skills develop. So, do it now!

WHATEVER THE PACE AND PRESSURE OF THE MODERN WORKPLACE, ONE TIMELESS PRINCIPLE HOLDS TRUE:

Fail to honor people, they fail to honor you.

Lao Tzu   6th century BC

Index